HOW TO FORM YOUR OWN CORPORATION WITHOUT A LAWYER FOR UNDER $50.00

By Ted Nicholas

Complete with Specimen Forms including
Certificate of Incorporation
Minutes, By-Laws—
All the information that is needed

Library of Congress Number 77-78063

International Standard Book Number 0-913864-46-3

Published by:
ENTERPRISE PUBLISHING CO., INC.
Two West Eighth Street
Wilmington, Delaware 19801

ACKNOWLEDGMENTS

I'd like to thank my friend, Sylvan N. Levy, Jr. for his useful suggestions after spending many hours reviewing the manuscript.

Additionally, the entire staff of Enterprise Publishing Co. has been of enormous assistance in the preparation of this book.

More Acknowledgments

In connection with this writing, special acknowledgment is given the Corporation Department, Secretary of State's office in Dover, Delaware and capable staff.

In particular, I deeply appreciate the efforts of the Assistant Secretary of State, Mr. Richard H. Caldwell, for his personal assistance and helpful comments in the review of the contents of this book.

Since the first printing of the hardcover edition in January 1973, Robert Reed, Secretary of State, appointed by Governor Sherman Tribbitt, Mr. Grover Biddle, the new Assistant Secretary of State and Mrs. Marie Shultie, Director, Corporation Department, and her staff, have been of enormous assistance in helping to process smoothly and efficiently the large volume of new corporations from all over the world that have been formed as a result of this book.

At the time of this printing, the present Secretary of State, Mr. Glenn C. Kenton, and the Assistant Secretary of State, O. E. Denny, appointed by Governor Pierre S. duPont, continue with the fine work that has been historically done by the Corporation Department.

T.N.

A BRIEF HISTORY OF THE CORPORATION

Much of American law has its origin in England. The Corporation as a legal entity under English law dates back to the late 14th century. In the early 1600's, again in England, a number of joint stock associations were formed in an attempt to gain the same advantage as chartered corporations. In all contractual dealings, these companies were able to offer their stockholders liability protection. Investors in such companies were as a result put in a more favorable position than partners whose liabilities for corporate debts is unlimited.

Corporations have been a part of North America's history for over 300 years. The Massachusetts Bay Company was chartered in 1629 by Charles I of England. Its purpose was to colonize the area near Massachusetts Bay. Subsequently, in 1630, it founded the city of Boston. The Hudson Bay Company of Canada was chartered in 1670 and continues to operate trading posts there today.

During the early stages of the American Republic, it took a special act of a state legislature to grant a corporate charter to a business enterprise. The first state to permit incorporation under a general law was New York in 1811.

By 1900, nearly all the states had constitutional provisions forbidding the granting of corporate charters by legislators.

Delaware was the first state to ratify the U.S. Constitution in 1787. The Delaware General Corporation law was adopted in 1899. Prior to this time corporate charters were granted by an act of the legislature. It was the pioneer State in creating an attractive climate for free enterprise. Many of the corporations during the Americas great industrial revolution during the 1800's were chartered in Delaware. This friendly and accommodating atmosphere toward business enterprises still exists today. Low taxes, fast service, simplified requirements, and the Court of Chancery, the only separate business court system in the U.S. combine to attract both small one-man corporations as well as large corporations to Delaware. One-third of the companies listed on American and New York Stock Exchanges are chartered in Delaware.

Corporations in America in the early stages were burdened with sharp restrictions on longevity and size. Terms fixed to a specific number of years, 20 to 50 years, were common. There were also ceilings on authorized capital. These and other limits were abandoned over a period of time.

In the 1700's a large part of world commerce was carried on by corporations. By the late 1800's corporations had multiplied enormously. Nearly every business owner that required capital, a union of large numbers of people or desired limited liability incorporated. The wealth and business holdings in the country to a great extent was and is controlled by them.

At present the States compete with each other to attract business to them. Some are more aggressive than others. This creates a healthy and unusual atmosphere. Many have attempted to model sections of their law on the General Corporation law of Delaware. However, while there are some similarities no State has been successful in achieving all Delaware's benefits.

Today, there are more than 1,700,000 active corporations. About 765,000 of these elected to be taxed like partnerships. According to the Wall Street Journal in excess of 30,000 new corporations are formed each month in North America.

As of this revised edition, this book is used by a measurable and growing number of them — 500 to 600 each month, or nearly 2% of all the corporations formed each month in the United States.

TABLE OF CONTENTS

Definition: A corporation is an entity created through the act of filing a document by an individual or group, known as articles of or certificate of incorporation with a state agency known as a "Corporation Department." This entity is recognized by law as a separate "person" existing in reality with limited liability, a separate tax status, the right to sue and be sued, the option of selling shares, and the capacity of succession.

"For many years, even decades, the Delaware General Corporation Law has been the pace-setter for American corporation statutes. Indeed, viewed realistically, Delaware Corporation Law is national corporation law."

"The fact is that states cannot effectively exert controls and restrictions even over enterprises organized under their own corporation statutes. If they attempt to do so, enterprises merely incorporate in some other state with a more 'liberal' statute since the federal system permits individuals to incorporate wherever they wish in order to do business on a local, state, national or international level."

From book, THE DELAWARE
GENERAL CORPORATION LAW
written by Ernest L. Folk, III,
Professor of Law, University of
Virginia and published for
Corporation Service Company by
Little, Brown and Company, Inc.
34 Beacon Street
Boston, MA 02106 $47.50

"Anyone may so arrange his affairs that his taxes shall be as low as possible: He is not bound to choose that pattern which will best pay the Treasury; there is not even a patriotic duty to increase one's taxes."

Judge Learned Hand

FOREWORD

The experience of the author is as a businessman and business consultant.

This book enables the reader to incorporate at the lowest possible cost. The forms that are necessary are in specimen type and are complete with instructions.

The author is a principal in The Company Corporation. This corporation provides various low cost services to persons who form a corporation (See Section VII).

Lawyer's fees for incorporating range from $300 to $3,000 or more. The system enables anyone in the United States to form a corporation without a lawyer at the lowest possible cost, and includes other money saving and tax saving ideas.

A little known fact is that in many states an individual can legally incorporate without the services of a lawyer. Lawyers provide important professional services to their clients. However, incorporation is a relatively simple task that does not require professional services. There are some lawyers who would like to charge lower fees for forming a corporation. State Bar Associations, however, provide recommended fee schedules for lawyers who do not like to go against these recommendations. Forming a corporation usually involves minimum legal fees of at least $300. This fee varies in accordance with the schedule or recommended fees of a particular State Bar Association. Average fees charged by lawyers tend to be higher than the recommended minimum.

Before this book was written, it was difficult for an individual to incorporate without a lawyer. The reason for this is that there was no publication on the matter written in everyday English. In addition, companies that assist individuals in forming a corporation work only through a lawyer who prepares the corporate documents. Legal fees for incorporation heretofore, were almost completely unavoidable.

Delaware is emphasized as the state in which to incorporate. Regardless of where a person lives or has a business, this book enables a person to incorporate and take advantage of Delaware Corporate Laws. In Delaware, anyone can form a corporation as long as he completes the forms provided for that purpose himself. The reason for this can be found in Section II.

Delaware is the State of incorporation for over 100,000 corporations. They range from small one man operations, to the largest ones in the United States. Because of the advantages to corporations of Delaware Corporate Laws, more than one-third of all corporations listed on the American and New York Stock Exchange are Delaware corporations. This is a much higher percentage than any other state.

The biggest percentage of the corporations formed in Delaware are headquartered in other states. The individuals who own these corporations almost never visit the state.

There are over twenty companies whose function is to act as "Registered Agent" and provide services including a Delaware mailing address for the corporations formed in Delaware.

In most cases, the needs of an individual or company who wishes to incorporate involve a simple corporate structure. The goal of this book is directed toward the simplest

1

and lowest cost method of forming a corporation. A person with a business of any type or size that wishes to incorporate and engage in any business endeavor anywhere in the United States can beneficially utilize the elements contained herein.

As of this edition the count of new corporations that have been formed by using this book has reached many thousands. Owners of these corporations reside in all 50 of the United States as well as in several other countries throughout the world.

Prices and fees quoted in this book may be increased without notice by the various States and other bodies, and should only be used as a guide.

ADVANTAGES OF INCORPORATING

SECTION I

Before one decides whether or not to incorporate, it is wise to review other alternatives.

There are two other fundamental ways to operate a business, individual proprietorship and partnership. Both have similar advantages and disadvantages. The main advantage is that they are slightly less expensive to start, since there are no incorporating fees. They are also a bit less formal.

In a corporation, periodic meetings and minutes of the meetings should be kept. This is a simple routine task. (See Section XXI)

ADVANTAGES OF PARTNERSHIPS AND PROPRIETORSHIPS

1. Somewhat lower cost to organize since there are no incorporating fees.

2. Less formality in record keeping.

3. The owners file one tax return.

4. Owners can deduct losses that might be incurred during the early life of a business from other personal income.

5. The limit of tax deductible contributions to "Keogh" type pension and profit sharing plans has been increased to $7,500. This has reduced the tax advantage of benefit plans previously available to a corporation.

6. Profits of a partnership, unlike dividends paid by a corporation are not subject to a second Federal income tax when distributed to the owners. However, whether this is an advantage, taxwise, depends on certain other factors, namely:

    a. The individual tax brackets of the owners as compared with that of the corporation.

    b. The extent to which double taxation of earnings of the corporation is eliminated by deductible salaries paid to owners and by retention of earnings in surplus.

SOME OF THE MAIN DISADVANTAGES OF PROPRIETORSHIPS AND PARTNERSHIPS ARE:

1. Unlimited personal liability. The owners are personally liable for all debts and judgments against the business, including liability in case of failure or other disaster.

2. In a partnership, each member can bind the other so that one partner can cause the other to be personally liable.

3. All profits are personally taxable to the owners at rates which are higher than corporate rates.

3

4. If the owner(s) dies or becomes incapacitated, the business often comes to a standstill.

5. The owner(s) do not have the full tax benefits of the tax deductible plans including pension and profit sharing that are available to a corporation.

THE ADVANTAGES OF INCORPORATING INCLUDE:

1. The personal liability of the founders is limited to the amount of money put into the corporation (with the exception of unpaid taxes).

2. If a business owner wishes to raise capital, a corporation is more attractive to investors who can purchase shares of stock in it for purposes of raising capital.

3. A corporation does not pay tax on monies it receives in exchange for its stock.

4. There are many more tax options available to corporations than to proprietorships or partnerships. One can set up pension, profit sharing, stock option plans that are favorable to the owners of the corporation.

5. A corporation can be continued more easily in the event of the death of its owners or principals.

6. Shares of a corporation can easily be distributed to family members.

7. The owners (shareholders) of a corporation that is discontinued due to its being unsuccessful can have all the advantages of being incorporated, yet be able to deduct up to $50,000 on an individual tax return or $100,000 on a joint return of money invested in the corporation from *personal* income. (See Section XVI)

8. The owner(s), stockholders, of a corporation can operate with all the advantages of a corporation, yet be taxed on personal income tax rates if this option provides a tax advantage. (See Section XV)

9. Owners can quickly transfer their ownership interest represented by shares of stock, without the corporation dissolving.

10. The corporation's capital can be expanded by issuing and selling additional shares of stock.

11. Shares of stock can be used for estate and family planning.

12. The corporation can ease the tax burden of its stockholders by accumulating its earnings. This is providing the accumulation is not unreasonable and is for a business purpose.

13. It is a separate legal "being," separate and apart from its owner(s) (stockholders). It can sue and be sued and can enter into contracts.

14. A corporation may own shares in another corporation and receive dividends, 85% of which are tax free. (However, see Personal Holding Companies, Section III.)

4

15. A corporation's Federal Income Tax Rates may be lower than the owner's individual tax rates, especially for a smaller company. As of January 1, 1979, the Income Tax Rates on companies are as follows:

Taxable Income	Rate of Tax
Up to 25,000	17%
25,000 — 50,000	20%
50,000 — 75,000	30%
75,000 — 100,000	40%
Over 100,000	46%

DISADVANTAGES OF INCORPORATING INCLUDE:

1. The owners of a corporation file two tax returns, individual and corporate. This may require added time and accounting expense. (The owner of a proprietorship files one return; a member of a partnership files two.)

2. Unless the net taxable income of a business is substantial, i.e., $25,000 or more, there may not be tax advantages. (However, in businesses where there is personal liability on the part of the owners, it may be desirable to incorporate even if the income is modest.)

3. Maintaining the corporate records may require added time. (See corporate forms, Section XII.)

4. If debt financing is obtained by a corporation, i.e., a loan from a bank, the fund source may require the personal guarantee by the owner(s) thereby eliminating the limited liability advantage of a corporation at least to the extent of the loan.

   NOTE: Probably the biggest single disadvantage to incorporating prior to the publication of this book, was the high initial cost.

REASONS FOR INCORPORATING IN DELAWARE

SECTION II

The advantages of incorporating in Delaware are:

1. There is *no* minimum capital requirement. A corporation can be organized with *zero* capital if desired. Many states require that a corporation have at least $1,000 in capital.

2. *One* person can hold the offices of President, Treasurer and Secretary and be all the directors. Many states require at least three officers and/or directors. Therefore, there is no need to bring other persons into a Delaware Corporation if the owner(s) does not desire it.

3. There is an established body of laws relevant to corporations that have been tested in the Delaware courts over the years. In the event of any legal matters that involve Delaware courts there is, therefore, a high degree of predictability in legal proceedings based on past history and experience. This can be meaningful to investors in a corporation. The Court of Chancery in Delaware is the only separate business court system in the United States, and has a long record of pro-management decisions.

4. There is no corporation income tax for corporations that are formed in Delaware but who do not do business in the state.

5. The Franchise Tax on corporations compares favorably with any other state.

6. Shares of stock owned by a person outside the state are not subject to any Delaware taxes.

7. A person can operate as the owner of a Delaware corporation anonymously if desired. (See Section XIV.)

8. One can form a corporation by mail and never visit the state, even to conduct Annual Meetings. Meetings can be held anywhere, at the option of the directors.

9. The Delaware Corporation Department welcomes new corporations and is organized to process them the same day they are received.

10. Delaware is the friendliest state to corporations. The reason is that the state depends on its Corporation Department as a prime source of revenue. The Corporation Revenue is exceeded only by Income Taxes. The State, therefore, depends on attracting a high volume of corporations. It has, historically, kept its laws and fees relevant to corporations favorable and at a low cost.

11. There is no Inheritance Tax on shares of stock held by non-residents. These shares are taxed only in the state of residence of the owners of the corporation.

12. Director(s) may fix a sales price on any stock that the corporation issues and wishes to sell.

13. Stockholders, directors, and/or committee members may act by unanimous written consent in lieu of formal meetings.

14. Director(s) may determine what part of consideration received for stock is capital.

15. Corporations can pay dividends out of profits as well as surplus.

16. Corporations can hold stocks, bonds, or securities of other corporations, real and personal property, within or without the state, without limitation as to amount.

17. Corporations may purchase shares of its own stock and hold, sell and transfer them.

18. Corporations may conduct different kinds of businesses in combination. If the corporate documents filed with Delaware have the broadest type "purpose clause" as outlined in this book, any business activity of any kind may be conducted. More than one type of business can be conducted by the same corporation without any changes in the documents filed with the state.

19. Corporations have perpetual existence (unless specified in its Certificate of Incorporation).

20. The director(s) has power to make or alter by-laws.

21. Stockholder liability is limited to stock held in the corporation (with exception of taxes and assuming the business is conducted in a legal manner).

22. Only one person acting as the incorporator is required, whereas many states require three.

Percentage of corporations listed on the New York and American Stock Exchanges which are incorporated in Delaware.

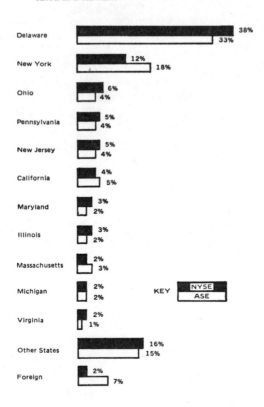

	NYSE	ASE
Delaware	38%	33%
New York	12%	18%
Ohio	6%	4%
Pennsylvania	5%	4%
New Jersey	5%	4%
California	4%	5%
Maryland	3%	2%
Illinois	3%	2%
Massachusetts	2%	3%
Michigan	2%	2%
Virginia	2%	1%
Other States	16%	15%
Foreign	2%	7%

KEY

TYPES OF SITUATIONS WHERE INDIVIDUALS MIGHT WISH TO INCORPORATE

SECTION III

A few examples of individuals who may wish to incorporate a business activity or profession planned or presently in operation are as follows:

1. A professional person (or partnership) such as an accountant, engineer, physician, dentist, architect, lawyer, etc.*

2. A franchised business owner.

3. A person or company planning to conduct a private or public stock offering.

4. A manufacturing service or retailing business. This includes a manufacturer's representative, a distributor (many of whom operate out of their homes). The list of types of situations include, but are not limited to: any type of retail operation, gas station, publishing, mail order operation, restaurant, beauty shop, loan company, etc.

5. A personal real estate investment such as an apartment building, store, or any commercial building project.

6. A business endeavor that would involve the ownership of one or more share holders (sometimes called partners).

7. An activity or organization that is organized for non-profit purposes; such as a foundation association, charitable organization, volunteer organization or fire company.

It often makes good sense both from a tax and personal liability standpoint, for certain interests of an individual, such as a real estate investment, to be incorporated separately.

NOTE: The Internal Revenue Service can deem certain corporations "Personal Holding Companies" and levy additional taxes beyond the normal level for a corporation.

Personal Holding Companies: Congress passed a law in 1934 to prevent avoidance of graduated income tax by placing investment funds in a corporation and retaining the income at the corporate level subject to the lower corporate income tax. This has often been called an "incorporated pocketbook."

In general terms a corporation is a personal holding company if five or fewer individuals own (directly or indirectly) more than 50% of the value of the outstanding stock and if 60% or more of the corporation's adjusted ordinary gross income is personal holding company income. Personal holding company income, in general consists of 'passive' income, i.e., with certain exceptions, it includes dividends, interest, annuities, gains from sale of securities, rent, etc.

For further information see Internal Revenue Code Section 543.

---

* For an indepth book on professional corporations, complete with necessary forms, see *How To Form Your Own Professional Corporation* by Ted Nicholas. Available at bookstores at $19.95 or direct from Enterprise Publishing Co., Two West Eighth Street, Wilmington, DE 19801.

CERTIFICATE OF INCORPORATION

SECTION IV

When a Delaware corporation is formed, a Certificate of Incorporation is filed with the Secretary of State's office and with the Recorder of Deeds. It is also necessary to have minutes of the first Director's Meeting, By-Laws of the corporation, stock certificates and corporate seal (specimen forms for everything except stock certificates and corporate seal are supplied in this book).

Any person or his Registered Agent (See Section VI) can file the Certificate of Incorporation.

An individual or his Registered Agent can also arrange to provide the corporation with a Delaware address. Preparation of minutes of the first director's meeting, by-laws, stock certificates and corporate seal all can be ordered and completed by the person incorporating. Minutes and by-laws in standard form can be adapted from this book and used for this purpose. A complete sample specimen is shown in Section V. Sample forms for by-laws and minutes are in Section XXI.

A very important element of the certificate is the Purpose Clause in paragraph three. The broadest clause enabling the corporation to engage in any business activity is used in this book. No matter what businesses the corporation engages in, this clause need not be changed. The broadest powers are given to the director(s) and officer(s). The only types of corporations to which this clause does not apply are institutions, schools, insurance companies, professional corporations, and banks.

1,000 shares of stock, which is the maximum number for the minimum state fee, is used in the sample specimen. This premise takes into consideration the Annual Corporate Franchise Fee which is only $20 for 1,000 shares. A person can have as many as 2,000 shares for the same initial fee. However, the Annual Fee is $24.20 instead of $20. If this number of shares *or any lesser number* is selected initially as the number authorized by the corporation, it can easily be changed at any time if more shares are to be issued later. More shares, stock splits or a new capital structure involve only a simple form to be filed with the state. A schedule showing the fees for these types of changes is available from the Secretary of State, Dover, Delaware. A Delaware Registered Agent can file the forms involving these changes or they can be filed by an individual residing anywhere in the United States.

FORMING THE CORPORATION WITHOUT ENGAGING A REGISTERED AGENT
SECTION V

Any person can form a Delaware corporation. The owner(s) never has to visit the state. Annual meetings may be held anywhere.

Below is the least costly way to accomplish the incorporation. (This approach, while the least costly, does not include the benefits of the services a registered agent can provide.)

The following are the steps involved:

1. Establish a street mailing address in Delaware. This can be a private home or office. (Without engaging a registered agent's services, to provide assistance, this is usually the most difficult problem to solve.) See Section VI.

2. Decide on whether to form a regular corporation or close corporation. (See Section V-A.) Prepare a certificate of incorporation using the same format as shown in specimen. The language in this certificate has been prepared by the Secretary of State, Dover, Delaware. Be sure to fill in the name and address of one incorporator who resides in any state.

    Send two signed copies of this certificate to the Secretary of State, Corporation Department, Townsend Building, Dover, Delaware 19901. Include a check in the amount of $45.00 which is the total cost of the incorporation. (This fee breaks down as follows: $25 for filing, receiving and indexing; $10 is the minimum State filing fee; and $10.00 for a certified copy.)

    If the corporate name you pick is not available you will be notified. Otherwise you will receive notice of the date that your corporation has been filed.

3. When you receive one certified copy of the certificate of incorporation plus a receipted bill from the State, this copy should then be filed with the Recorder of Deeds office in the county where the street mailing address of the Corporation is located. There are three counties in Delaware. The addresses for the Recorder of Deeds offices in the three counties are as follows:

    Kent County — County Courthouse, Dover, Delaware 19901
    Sussex County — Box 505, Georgetown, Delaware 19947
    New Castle County — 800 French Street, Wilmington, DE 19801

    Enclose a check for $10.00. (The charge is *$5.00 per page* submitted, minimum $10.00 to record a one page certificate and the certification page. Conventional certificates prepared and typed on legal size paper are from four to ten pages, costing the person filing from $20 to $50. This is the reason that all the certificates of incorporation except the non-stock are printed on *one page* and are available from The Company Corporation.)

    In some states, other than Delaware, a similar incorporation procedure applies. If a reader is interested for any reason in forming a non-Delaware corporation, he can obtain specific information by writing to the Corporation

Department, Secretary of State in any state. However, no state has all the benefits of incorporating in Delaware.

Specimen forms are provided in Section XXI for by-laws and minutes of the first meeting.

There are also legal stationery companies that can supply a complete kit of the above forms, at a cost ranging from $30 to $50. A corporate seal and stock certificates cost $10 to $20.

The Company Corporation provides a "kit" including a corporate seal, stock certificates, forms for minutes for Section 1244 of the Internal Revenue Code (see Section VII) for $39.95.

If you prefer to engage a registered agent to act in your behalf, such services can easily be obtained. (See Section VI)

CERTIFICATE OF INCORPORATION
of
JOHN DOE, INC.

FIRST. The name of this corporation is _(Repeat name exactly as above)_ JOHN DOE, INC.

SECOND. Its registered office in the State of Delaware is to be located at _____ 725 Market Street _____ in the _____ City of Wilmington _____ , County of ____ New Castle ____ _____ . The registered agent in charge thereof is _(name and address of your registered agent)_ The Company Corporation _____ at ____ same as above ____ .

THIRD. The nature of the business and, the objects and purposes proposed to be transacted, promoted and carried on, are to do any or all the things herein mentioned, as fully and to the same extent as natural persons might or could do, and in any part of the world, viz:

"The purpose of the corporation is to engage in any lawful act or activity for which corporations may be organized under the General Corporation Law of Delaware."

FOURTH. The amount of the total authorized capital stock of this corporation is __1,000__ _____ shares of _____ no _____ Par Value.

FIFTH. The name and mailing address of the incorporator is as follows:

NAME: ADDRESS:

(Leave blank if using The Company Corporation as agent, otherwise, your name and address.)

SIXTH. The powers of the incorporator are to terminate upon filing of the certificate of incorporation, and the name(s) and mailing address(es) of persons who are to serve as director(s) until the first annual meeting of stockholders or until their successors are elected and qualify are as follows:

Name and address of director(s)

John Doe, 1 Main Street, Atlantis, Calif.   Fill in name(s)

Jane Doe, 1 Main Street, Atlantis, Calif.   and address(es)

SEVENTH. The Directors shall have power to make and to alter or amend the By-Laws; to fix the amount to be reserved as working capital and to authorize and cause to be executed, mortgages and liens without limit as to the amount, upon the property and franchise of the Corporation.

With the consent in writing, and pursuant to a vote of the holders of a majority of the capital stock issued and outstanding, the Directors shall have the authority to dispose, in any manner, of the whole property of this corporation.

The By-Laws shall determine whether and to what extent the accounts and books of this corporation, or any of them shall be open to the inspection of the stockholders; and no stockholder shall have any right of inspecting any account, or book or document of this Corporation, except as conferred by the law or the By-Laws, or by resolution of the stockholders.

The stockholders and directors shall have power to hold their meetings and keep the books, documents and papers of the Corporation outside of the State of Delaware, at such places as may be from time to time designated by the By-Laws or by resolution of the stockholders or directors, except as otherwise required by the laws of Delaware.

It is the intention that the objects, purposes and powers specified in the Third paragraph hereof shall, except where otherwise specified in said paragraph, be nowise limited or restricted by reference to or inference from the terms of any other clause or paragraph in this certificate of incorporation, but that the objects, purposes and powers specified in the Third paragraph and in each of the clauses or paragraphs of this charter shall be regarded as independent objects, purposes and powers.

I, THE UNDERSIGNED, for the purpose of forming a Corporation under the laws of the State of Delaware, do make, file and record this Certificate and do certify that the facts herein are true; and I have accordingly hereunto set my hand.

DATED AT: _____

State of _____

County of_____

(Leave blank unless you are incorporator.)

_____
(Signature of person named in Fifth Article or signature of officer of corporation named in Fifth Article.)

13

A CLOSE CORPORATION

SECTION V—A

A close corporation is a corporation whose Certificate of Incorporation contains the basic elements contained in a standard Delaware corporation and, in addition, provides that:

1. All the corporation's issued stock shall be held by not more than a specified number of persons, not exceeding thirty.

2. All the issued stock shall be subject to one or more restrictions on transfer. The most widely used restriction is one which obligates a shareholder to offer to the corporation or other holders of shares of the corporation a prior opportunity to be exercised within a reasonable time; to acquire the restricted securities.

Sometimes other restrictions are included in the Certificate of Incorporation which:

A. Obligates the corporation for any holder of shares of the corporation to purchase the shares which are the subject of an agreement regarding the purchase and sale of the restricted shares; or

B. Requires the corporation or shareholders of the corporation to consent to any proposed transfer of the restricted shares; or

C. Prohibits the transfer of restricted shares to designated persons or classes of persons; if such designation is not unreasonable.

D. Any restriction on the transfer of shares of a corporation for the purpose of maintaining its status as an electing small business corporation under Subchapter "S" of the Internal Revenue Code is presumed to be for a reasonable purpose.

E. Another unique feature is that the certificate of incorporation of a close corporation may provide that the business of the corporation shall be managed by the stockholders. No directors need be elected so that there are no directors meetings necessary. This provision has the effect of eliminating the formality of having directors meetings. Under this feature, the shareholders of the corporation have the powers and responsibilities that directors would normally have.

A close corporation is not permitted to make a "public" offering of its shares within the meaning of the Securities Act of 1933.

If a person who is running a corporation wishes to limit shareholders in number and who also wishes that he and/or other shareholders have the first opportunity to buy shares from a selling shareholder, a close corporation is the ideal type of form. This first option to buy shares of stock can be the key to preventing undersirable persons from becoming shareholders in a corporation.

14

An existing Delaware corporation can also elect to be a close corporation if two-thirds of the shareholders vote in favor of it. An amendment to this effect is filed with the Secretary of State in Dover, Delaware.

A close corporation can change its status to a regular or "open" corporation by filing a certificate of amendment with the Secretary of State.

On the following pages is a specimen copy that can be used as a guide should a person wish to form a close corporation. It contains the provisions referred to in paragraphs 1, 2, and E.

As with other Delaware corporations, the certificate of incorporation can be filed using any address initially. However, it is preferable to have these filed through a registered agent since a Delaware mailing address is necessary.

CERTIFICATE OF INCORPORATION
of
ABC CORPORATION (Name of Company)

A CLOSE CORPORATION

FIRST. The name of this Corporation is (Repeat proposed name here) ABC Corporation

SECOND. Its registered office in the State of Delaware is to be located at (Delaware mailing address or registered agent's address) i.e., 725 Market St., City of Wilmington

County of New Castle . The registered agent in charge thereof is (Fill in name of registered agent, i.e., The Company Corporation, otherwise use your name.)

address "same as above".

THIRD. The nature of the business and, the objects and purposes proposed to be transacted, promoted and carried on, are to engage in any lawful act or activity for which corporations may be organized under the General Corporation Law of Delaware.

FOURTH. The amount of total authorized capital stock of the corporation is divided into (Put number of shares desired) i.e., 1,000 shares of no-par value (unless desire to establish a par value) .

FIFTH. The name and mailing address of the incorporator is as follows:
(Leave blank if using The Company Corporation, otherwise use your name and address)

SIXTH. The powers of the incorporator are to terminate upon filing of the certificate of incorporation, and the name and mailing addresses of the persons who are to serve as managing stockholder(s) until their successors are elected are as follows:

Name and address of managing stockholder(s)

Fill in name(s)
and address(es)

SEVENTH. All of the corporations issued stock, exclusive of treasury shares, shall be held of record by not more than thirty (30) persons.

EIGHTH. All of the issued stock of all classes shall be subject to the following restriction on transfer permitted by Section 202 of the General Corporation Law.

Each stockholder shall offer to the Corporation or to other stockholders of the corporation a thirty (30) day "first refusal" option to purchase his stock should he elect to sell his stock.

NINTH. The corporation shall make no offering of any of its stock of any class which would constitute a "public offering" within the meaning of the United States Securities Act of 1933, as it may be amended from time to time.

I, THE UNDERSIGNED, for the purpose of forming a corporation under the laws of the State of Delaware do make, file and record this certificate, and do certify that the facts herein stated are true; and I have accordingly hereunto set my hand.

DATED AT:

(Signature of person or officer of corporation named in Fifth Article)
(Leave blank if using The Company Corporation)

16

REGISTERED AGENTS

SECTION VI

In Delaware there are more than thirty companies that provide "registered agent" services to corporations. There is a list of some of these companies in Section VI. One of the main functions of these companies is to provide a street address for corporations. All corporations formed in Delaware are required to have a mailing address in the state. These service companies that can provide this (and other services) are known as *Registered Agents.*

Annual fees charged by registered agents for providing a Delaware address range from $75 to $250 per year. One of the largest registered agents (who owns several registered agent companies) charges $150 per year. If a lawyer's services are used, there are additional fees of $300—$3,000. Registered agents generally charge an additional fee of $60 to $300 for the initial formation of a corporation.

One company, The Company Corporation, charges only $25* per calendar year during the first year for their annual registered agent service. This modest fee is less than that charged by others. This fee increases to $35 for the second year and $50 the third year.

There is *no initial fee* charged for the formation of the corporation. *No* legal fees are necessary since *customers* of The Company Corporation *complete the forms themselves.* No counseling service is provided or needed if the forms are completed by the person who is forming the corporation.

Service is provided in a highly confidential manner as well as a speedy one. Upon receipt of forms, corporation name is reserved with Secretary of State the *same* day. Forms are forwarded within 24 hours.

Potential savings using The Company Corporation for the initial formation of the corporation is up to $3,000 and up to $250 a year on an annual basis.

The Company Corporation operates differently than other registered agents. It operates on a volume basis and advertises for its customers on a direct basis. Its fees are substantially less than its competitors. All "middle man" type fees are eliminated.

The Company Corporation will provide services to customers referred by lawyers but does not require this. No other registered agent serves customers who are not lawyer referred.

All that is required is that a certificate of incorporation and signed Confidential Information form be completed by the customer and sent to The Company Corporation. Certificate is then forwarded to the appropriate places.

No legal advice or counseling is provided by The Company Corporation. Administerial functions only are provided. No review or advice on the form itself can be given. However, if the form is complete (instructions are contained herein) *none is necessary.* If for any reason the certificate of incorporation is not accepted by the Secretary of State in Dover, Delaware it is returned without comment by The Company Corporation with any of the Secretary of State's comments.

*Prices and fees are subject to change without notice.

In addition to providing a permanent street address in Delaware, The Company Corporation, unlike any other registered agent, provides the following services at *no* cost to its customers:

INITIAL SERVICE

1. Act as registered agent and provide a mailing address in Delaware. The Company Corporation provides a mailing address for the purpose of receiving and forwarding all legal documents, not general mail delivery. General mail forwarding can be arranged for an additional fee.

2. Furnish the incorporator. (Certificate of incorporation can be completed but unsigned if desired.)

3. Forward the certificate of incorporation with the Corporation Department in Dover, Delaware for filing.

4. File a copy of the Certificate of Incorporation in the Recorder of Deeds office.

5. Prepare checks for payment of initial recording fees to the State of Delaware.

6. Reserve corporate name the same day request is received from customer.

7. Order printed stock certificates, corporate seal and forms for minutes and by-laws, if this option is desired by client.

8. Supply the appropriate forms for qualifying the Delaware Corporation in any other state in the United States at the nominal handling charge — $.50 each upon request.

CONTINUING SERVICES

9. Act as registered agent and provide a mailing address in Delaware.

10. Forward the corporation annual report form to the Secretary of State, Dover, Delaware. Once each year the Secretary of State, Dover, Delaware sends to the Delaware mailing address of every corporation chartered in the State, an annual report form. The Company Corporation forwards this to its customers. It is completed by the customer and sent back to The Company Corporation who then forwards it to the Secretary of State, Dover, Delaware for filing.

11. Referral service to competent Delaware lawyers, if legal counseling or advice is requested on any corporate matter (since the volume of corporate activity is so great in Delaware, many capable lawyers practice there.)

12. Assist in locating facilities for annual meetings if the client wishes to have them and/or hold them in Delaware.

13. Receive legal documents served on the corporation in Delaware, including law suits, and forward these to the business address of the corporation.

14. Publish a periodic newsletter at least four times a year dealing with helpful business ideas that can save money. Also other services that The Company Corporation makes available to its customers are described in the newsletter. Other services through affiliated companies include design of company logos, simplified bookkeeping systems, tax deductible group and individual insurance plans, helpful books and tapes, and advertising agency assistance.

In addition, The Company Corporation will furnish upon request the Delaware fee schedule for filing forms with the state. These include, but are not limited to: increases of number of shares of stock, new classes of stock, amending certificates of incorporation, dissolutions, etc.

A partial list of companies in Delaware that are available to provide services to corporations, including acting as Registered Agent are listed as follows:

No initial fee for filing corporate documents
No legal fees necessary
Annual Fee $25.00 first calendar year
$35.00 second calendar year
$50.00 third year and thereafter

THE COMPANY CORPORATION
CORPORATION CENTER
725 MARKET ST.
WILMINGTON, DE 19801

Initial Fee $60-$300 for filing corporate documents. Legal Fees $300-$3,000 (most of these companies require that clients be referred by lawyer), Annual Fee $75-$250.

American Corporation Co.
506 Beneficial Building
Wilmington, Delaware 19801

American Guaranty & Trust Co.
3801 Kennett Pike
Greenville Center
Wilmington, Delaware 19807

Boat Charter & Documentation, Inc.
725 Market Street
Wilmington, Delaware 19801

Capital Trust Co. of Delaware
1105 N. Market Street
Wilmington, Delaware 19801

Colonial Charter Co.
1102 West Street
Wilmington, Delaware 19801

Corporation Company of Delaware
1105 N. Market Street
Wilmington, Delaware 19801

Corporation Guarantee & Trust Co.
901 Market Street
722 Bank of Delaware Bldg.
Wilmington, Delaware 19801

Corporate Registry Company
Delaware Trust Bldg.
900 Market Street
Wilmington, Delaware 19801

Corporate Service Co.
1105 N. Market Street
Wilmington, Delaware 19801

Corporate Trust Co. (The)
1105 N. Market Street
Wilmington, Delaware 19801

Delaware Charter Co.
1105 N. Market Street
Wilmington, Delaware 19801

Delaware Charter Guarantee & Trust Co.
1105 N. Market Street
Wilmington, Delaware 19801

Delaware Corporation Agency
300 Market Tower
901 Market Street
Wilmington, Delaware 19801

Delaware Corporation Service (The)
1105 N. Market Street
Wilmington, Delaware 19801

Delaware Enterprises, Inc.
26 The Green
Dover, Delaware 19901

Delaware Incorporators Trust Co.
1105 N. Market Street
Wilmington, Delaware 19801

Initial Fee $60-$300 for filing corporate documents. Legal Fees $300-$3,000 (these companies require that clients be referred by lawyer), Annual Fee $75-$250.

Delaware Registration Trust Co.
900 Market Street
Wilmington, Delaware 19801

Professional Corporation Co.
725 Market Street
Wilmington, Delaware 19801

Incorporating Services, Ltd.
26 The Green
Dover, Delaware 19901

Registrar and Transfer Co.
306 South State Street
Dover, Delaware 19901

Incorporators of Delaware
48 The Green
Dover, Delaware 19901

States Charters Corporation
The Green
Dover, Delaware 19901

Prentice-Hall Corp. System, Inc. (The)
229 South State Street
Dover, Delaware 19901

United States Corporation Co.
306 South State St.
Dover, DE 19901

SECTION VII

Any registered agent listed in this book may assist in filing forms for incorporating and providing other services to corporations. The Company Corporation provides their services in a different manner and at lower cost than any other company; also, it will assist you in incorporating in the State of Delaware, or any other State of the Union.

The Company Corporation charges no fee for initial administerial services in filing the certificate of incorporation with the State of Delaware, providing that The Company Corporation is appointed registered agent. Other registered agents charge up to $300 for initial incorporating services; in addition to legal fees charged by a lawyer. The annual fee for engaging The Company Corporation is $25 during the first year and there are no legal fees. The fee gradually increases to $35.00 the second year and $50 the third year and thereafter. This modest graduating fee is designed to help keep costs as low as possible during the corporation's early formative years.

The only other initial cost to the incorporator is Delaware State fees as follows:

$25 covers the cost of filing, receiving and indexing the certificate; $10 is the minimum State Tax (authorized capitalization not exceeding $100,000 or 2,000 no-par shares; 1,000 shares, as previously suggested, results in the lowest fees); $10.00 for a certified copy from the State, and $10.00 for a *one page* certificate, or a total of $55.00. The aggregate amount paid to The Company Corporation at the time the Charter is filed is $80.00. This includes first year annual fee of $25 for registered agent service.

Most certificates of incorporation run unnecessarily to four or more pages costing $20 or more just to file. The forms in this book, all on one page except non-stock, cost only $5.00 per page ($10.00 minimum) to file with the Recorder of Deeds. Copy used in the certificates of incorporation contained in this book has been reproduced from forms supplied by the Secretary of State, Dover, Delaware.

Minutes of the first meeting and by-laws may be adapted from the samples in this book and used for the new corporation. Stock certificates and corporate seal are available from stationery stores.

As an option to its customers, The Company Corporation makes available the following Corporate Kit:

1. Vinyl covered Record Book to hold corporate records (with extra large holes) size 10-5/8 x 2-1/4 x 11-3/4, corporate name printed on gold insert.

2. Metal corporate seal imprinted with corporate name 1-5/8" diameter in a zipper pouch. This can be used on various documents.

3. Twenty (20) lithographed stock certificates of one class of stock all *numbered* and *printed* with *corporate* name and *capitalization*. (If more than one class of stock, you may request price.)

4. Pre-printed minutes and by-law forms to fit into above book.

5. Tax shelter under Section 1244 of the Internal Revenue Code. Complete set of forms and instructions make it easy to obtain benefits.

The total minimum cost for utilizing The Company Corporation as a registered agent in the State of Delaware is $80.00. With the above optional and useful material, the additional cost is $39.95, making a total of $119.95. Details and costs for incorporating in other states are available on request.

Delaware State & County Fees	Incorporating Fee—Using The Company Corporation first Year's* Registered Agent Fee	TOTAL
$55.00	$25.00	$ 80.00
	Optional Corporate Kit	39.95
Total payable to The Company Corporation—including Kit		$ 119.95**

In rare cases there may be a need for a corporation that differs slightly from the examples in this book, involving more than one class of stock, more shares, etc. The Company Corporation will furnish quotations of what the State of Delaware filing fees are for any type corporation. In no case does The Company Corporation charge more than the $25 annual registered agent fee for filing initial documents as long as they are completed by the customer.

The Company Corporation cannot furnish personal counsel or advise or answer questions to inquiries that involve interpretations or opinions of law.

---

* Annual registered agent fee is payable each *calendar* year. Calendar year begins on January 1st.
** All prices and fees subject to change without notice.

CONFIDENTIAL INFORMATION FORM

(To accompany completed Certificate of Incorporation form)

1. Name of Corporation: _____
   (A) Alternative name if above name is reserved or already being used by another corporation
   _____

2. Nature of business the company will transact: _____
   _____

3. No. of shares of common stock (up to 1,000 at lowest cost) _____
   (These shares shall be NO PAR VALUE unless otherwise specified)
   If par value shares, indicate what par:_____

4. Where is principal office outside of Delaware: _____

5. Number of Directors: _____

6. Date and place of annual meeting of stockholders: _____
   _____

7. Date and place of regular meetings of Directors:_____
   _____

8. Name(s) and address(es) of Director(s): _____
   _____

9. Names of officer(s): (One person may hold all offices)
   PRESIDENT _____ VICE PRESIDENT_____
   SECRETARY_____ TREASURER _____

10. Any special instructions:_____

11. Name of Applicant: _____ Telephone: _____
    No. & Street_____
    City, State, Zip:_____

    Enclosed is a check payable to The Company Corporation in the amount of: _____ $80.00*
    _____ $119.95* (includes corporate kit) With deluxe genuine leather corporate kit total amount is
    _____ $169.50* (Add $10.00 postage and handling for air mail delivery; $15.00 Canada air mail;
    $20.00 Foreign air mail.)

    NOTE: For rapid 48 hour service, enclose a certified check, treasurers check, or money order.
    Otherwise allow fourteen (14) days.

    Where did you purchase this book?
    From an advertisement in _____ Bookstore _____
    Referred by _____ Other _____
    Address _____
    Have you been incorporated before?   Yes   No   At what cost _____

12. I certify that The Company Corporation has provided no personal counsel or advice with regard to
    the above corporation, and that I have completed the enclosed Certificate of Incorporation myself.

    _____ (Signature)

*These amounts include the first calendar year registered agent fee of $25.00.

The Company Corporation will provide a complete "kit" that includes:

1. **Handsome gold stamping** on black vinyl binder and slip case to protect records. Your corporate name printed on gold insert for spine of binder.

2. **Corporate Seal** — fits in your pocket, or can be kept in pouch inside binder. Seal often required for completion of legal documents, such as: leases and purchase agreements. Your corporate name and year of incorporation permanently etched into dies which create a raised impression on any paper. (Seal separately is $15.00 for up to 40 characters.)

3. **Minutes and by-laws** printed on three hole paper for easy permanent record. Complete forms included for any Delaware corporation, along with instructions.

4. **20 lithographed stock certificates** printed with your corporate name on each certificate. Rich background design. Printing also includes number of shares authorized by corporation. (Additional stock certificates can be purchased. Minimum purchase is 26 @ $13.50 total; 27-100 @ $.65 each; over 100 @ $.25 each.)

5. **Celluloid tab index separators** make it easy to turn to any section in binder.

6. **Stock Transfer Ledger** to keep an accurate and complete record of any stock sold in your corporation.

7. **Information on Section 1244 of the Internal Revenue Code.** Useful forms with instructions that enable shareholders to qualify for favorable and important tax benefits. (There is an additional charge of $5.95 for complete Section 1244 materials.)

8. **Extra blank pages** for any business purpose. (Additional blanks @ $3.00 per 100.)

Overall size is **12" x 10" x 1½"** — A beautiful addition to any library or desk. All the above for $39.95, delivered anywhere in the world.

A Deluxe Genuine Leather Binder and Corporate Kit with corporate name stamped in gold and containing all of the above is available at $94.95.

EXISTING CORPORATIONS THAT WISH TO CHANGE REGISTERED AGENTS

SECTION VII — A

In order for an existing *Delaware* corporation to obtain the advantages offered by The Company Corporation, a simple form is all that is necessary. If a person wishes to change agents the total cost to that corporation the first year is $50.00. This is the actual filing cost that is paid to the State of Delaware. This is less than existing corporations are charged by their present Registered Agent each year. The fee is $40.00 to file the form with the Secretary of State and $10.00 to the Recorder of Deeds for a total of $50.00.

The Company Corporation will provide its registered agent services *at no cost* during the first calendar year to existing corporations. Thereafter, its annual fee is $50. This is an annual savings of at least $25 and up to $200.

A specimen of the Delaware form that makes it possible to change registered agents is on the next page.

If a reader wishes to avail himself of this low cost service, write The Company Corporation for a copy of this form in duplicate. By mailing this form and completed Confidential Information form with a check for $50.00 (payable to The Company Corporation) the certification document will be forwarded to the Secretary of State's office in Dover, Delaware for filing.

If the corporation has its present office in Kent or Sussex County prepare an additional copy of the form and add $7.50 to the amount, making a total of $57.50.

CERTIFICATE OF CHANGE OF LOCATION OF REGISTERED
OFFICE AND REGISTERED AGENT
OF

_____

The board of directors of the _____
a corporation of Delaware, on this _____ day of _____
A.D. 19_____ do hereby resolve and order that the location of the registered office of this
corporation within this State be, and the same hereby is _____
street, in the City of_____, in the County of_____

The name of the registered agent therein and in charge thereof upon whom
process against this corporation may be served is _____

The _____, a corporation of Delaware,
doth hereby certify that the foregoing is a true copy of a resolution adopted by the board of
directors at a meeting held as herein stated.

IN WITNESS WHEREOF, said corporation has caused this certificate to be signed
by its President and Attested by its Secretary, and its corporate seal to be hereto affixed,
the _____ day of _____ A.D. 19_____.

By _____

(SEAL)   PRESIDENT

ATTEST:

_____

SECRETARY

STATE FEE FOR QUALIFYING
DELAWARE CORPORATIONS IN OTHER STATES

SECTION VIII

A Delaware corporation that has all or most of its activities in another state is supposed to register the corporation in that state. Many Delaware corporations fail to register in other states. The hazard in not qualifying is usually a small fine and payment of a registration fee. Also, the unqualified Delaware corporation may not be able to use the courts of another state. Anyone can write to the Secretary of State in any State to determine its policy on "foreign" corporations who have not registered within that state.

In the following pages are the fees and taxes charged by each state for "qualifying" a Delaware corporation in another state as a "Foreign" corporation. The list of fees is broken down into initial and continuing fees, i.e., if a Minnesota resident has his business in Minnesota and forms a Delaware corporation, he is supposed to pay the home state a fee for "qualifying" a "foreign" corporation. The qualification procedure for "foreign" corporations is simple and can be accomplished at any time. A Delaware registered agent can file a copy of the certificate of incorporation with any particular state or states anytime during the life of the corporation. The Company Corporation provides this service to its customers at a forwarding cost of $5.00.

There are businesses that legally circumvent paying fees to home state by establishing that they are "doing business" in Delaware and not in another state.

Examples would include corporations that receive and ship materials from Delaware, mail order businesses who use a Delaware office, corporations that own property in Delaware and franchise or licensing companies who transact all contracts and orders in Delaware.

As to out of state residents who incorporate in Delaware, the Secretary of State's office in Dover, Delaware does not notify any other state as to who the new Delaware corporation owners or shareholders are or in what state they have a business office.

On the following pages there are fees for all states outlined. Initial filing fees, pages 28-31, minimum annual fees pages 33-35. The fees charged by the various states are, of course, subject to change. If an additional certified copy of a Delaware Certificate of Incorporation is required by another state, Delaware's fee is $11.00 for a one page certificate. A certificate of good standing, required by some states, is also $10.00.

SECTION IX

Each state's Corporation Department assesses fees to all corporations "foreign" to that state:

STATE
ALABAMA*

Filing certified copy of Articles of Incorporation	$10.00
Initial Tax (minimum)	25.00
Annual Franchise Tax	25.00
Fee for annual Permit (minimum)	5.00
Filing Designation of Agent	10.00
Total Minimum Fee	$75.00

ALASKA**

Initial fee based on authorized capital stock (minimum)	$ 25.00
Filing appointment of Commissioner of Commerce as agent	5.00
Annual Corporation Tax	100.00
Total Minimum Fee	$130.00

ARIZONA***

Filing copy of charter	$ 1.00
Filing Appointment of Agent License fee	65.00
Total Minimum Fee	$66.00

ARKANSAS*

On capital stock represented (minimum)	$18.00
Agent Fee	3.00
Name Registration	15.00
Total Minimum Fee	$36.00

CALIFORNIA**

Filing Statement	$350.00
Franchise Tax (minimum)	200.00
Total Minimum Fee	$550.00

COLORADO*

Filing application for, and issuing certificate of authority	$ 50.00
Initial License Fee	50.00
Total Minimum Fee	$100.00

STATE
CONNECTICUT**

Initial license fee	$100.00
Filing application for certificate of authority	20.00
Total Minimum Fee	$120.00

DISTRICT OF COLUMBIA*

Filing and indexing application	$22.00

FLORIDA*

Par Value Shares $4.00/share through $125,000 $1.00/share on additional value	
No Par Value Shares Florida assesses $.50/share through 1,250 shares and $.10/share for 1,251 through 10,000 shares to compute tax.	
Tax on capital employed or to be employed (minimum)	$30.00
Filing Designation of Agent	3.00
Issuing permit to do business	15.00
Total Minimum Fee	$48.00

GEORGIA*

Filing application and issuing Certificate of Authority	$100.00
Filing Annual Report	5.00
Total Minimum Fee	$105.00

HAWAII***

Qualification Fee	$ 50.00
Annual License Fee (prorated from 1st of month in which business is begun to following July 1st)	100.00
Total Minimum Fee	$150.00

STATE

IDAHO**

Filing articles of incorporation (minimum)	$20.00
Filing and recording Designation	4.00
Fees for certifying qualification forms (minimum, approx.)	3.00
Issuing certificate of qualification	6.00
Annual License Tax (minimum, but prorated)	20.00
To County Recorder	3.00
Total Minimum Fee	**$56.00**

ILLINOIS*

Filing Application	$ 75.00
Initial License Fee (minimum)	.50
Franchise Tax (minimum, but prorated)	25.00
Recording (approx.)	7.25
Total Minimum Fee	**$107.75**

INDIANA*

Filing Application (minimum)	$30.00
Issuing Certificate of Admission	6.00
Total Minimum Fee	**$36.00**

IOWA*

Filing Application	$20.00

KANSAS**

Application Fee	$50.00
Capitalization fee (minimum)	10.00
Filing and recording fee to Secretary of State	3.00
Recording Fee to Register of Deeds	7.00
Total Minimum Fee	**$70.00**

KENTUCKY*

Filing certified copy of Articles of Incorporation	$25.00
Recording certified copy of Articles of Incorporation	10.00
Recording Statement of Office and Agent	1.00
Total Minimum Fee	**$36.00**

STATE

LOUISIANA*

On authorized capital stock employed (minimum)	$10.00
Incorporation fee: filing and recording	7.00
Filing application for certificate of authority (approx.)	5.00
Issuing certificate of qualification	5.00
Total Minimum Fee	**$27.00**

MAINE**

Filing Power of Attorney Filing Foreign Corporation Certificate	$100.00
Total Minimum Fee	**$100.00**

MARYLAND

Filing certified copy of charter Certificate of Compliance	$50.00
Total Minimum Fee	**$50.00**

MASSACHUSETTS*

Filing charter and by-laws	$200.00

MICHIGAN**

Franchise Fee (minimum)	$25.00
For filing and examining certified copy of charter	10.00
Total Minimum Fee	**$35.00**

MINNESOTA*

Initial License Fee	$125.00
Filing Application for and issuing Certificate of Authority	19.00
Recording fee	2.00
Total Minimum Fee	**$146.00**

MISSISSIPPI*

Filing Application for Certificate of Authority (minimum)	$25.00
Filing Certified Copy of Appointment of Registered Agent	5.00
Total Minimum Fee	**$30.00**

STATE

MISSOURI**

On proportion of capital represented (minimum)	$50.00
Issuing certificate	13.00
Total Minimum Fee	**$63.00**

MONTANA*

Filing Application for Certificate of Authority and issuing Certificate of Authority	$20.00
License Fee	50.00
Total Minimum Fee	**$70.00**

NEBRASKA**

Filing Application for Certificate of Authority	$50.00
Issuing Certificate of Authority	1.00
Recording Application and Certificate of Authority	2.00
Total Minimum Fee	**$53.00**

NEVADA*

Filing certificate of incorporation (minimum) Certifying copy of charter Filing List of Officers and Directors Filing copy of certificate of incorporation with County Clerk	$50.00
Total Minimum Fee	**$50.00**

NEW HAMPSHIRE*

Registration fee	$100.00

NEW JERSEY**

Filing Application for Certificate of Authority	$165.00

NEW MEXICO*

Filing fee based on authorized capital stock (minimum)	$25.00
Filing Application for Certificate of Authority	5.00
Filing first Annual Report	5.00
Minimum Franchise tax	10.00
Total Minimum Fee	**$45.00**

NEW YORK**

Certificate of Authority	$110.00

STATE

NORTH CAROLINA*

Fee on authorized capital stock (minimum)	$45.00
Filing fee	1.80
Total Minimum Fee	**$46.80**

NORTH DAKOTA*

Initial License Fee	$ 75.00
Filing Application for Certificate of Authority	25.00
Total Minimum Fee	**$100.00**

OHIO**

Filing fee	$75.00

OKLAHOMA*

Initial Fee (on capital invested) (minimum) Filing Articles of Domestication and issuing Certificate of Domestication	$18.00
Total Minimum Fee	**$18.00**

OREGON**

Filing Application for Certificate of Authority	$ 50.00
Annual License Fee	200.00
Total Minimum Fee	**$250.00**

PENNSYLVANIA**

Filing Application for Certificate of Authority	$150.00
Total Minimum Fee	**$150.00**

PUERTO RICO*

Filing certified Copy of Charter	$100.00
Initial License fee	25.00
Issuing Certificate of Filing of Charter	5.00
Total Minimum Fee	**$130.00**

RHODE ISLAND*

Filing Fee	$20.00

STATE
SOUTH CAROLINA*

Filing Application for Certificate of Authority	$ 5.00
Additional tax on Capital (minimum)	40.00
Total Minimum Fee	$45.00

SOUTH DAKOTA*

Filing Application for Certificate of Authority (minimum)	$50.00

TENNESSEE**

Filing Application for Certificate of Authority	$300.00
Filing Designation of Agent	5.00
Total Minimum Fee	$305.00

TEXAS***

Filing Application for Certificate of Authority	$500.00
Nonprofit Corporation	$ 25.00

UTAH*

Filing application for and issuing Certificate of Authority	$25.00
License fee (minimum)	25.00
Total Minimum Fee	$50.00

VERMONT

For issuing Certificate of Authority	$60.00

VIRGINIA*

Par Value Shares Fee on authorized capital stock ($50,000 or less $30; 60 cents per $1,000 up to $1,000,000, etc.)	$60.00
No Par Value Shares Assessed at $100/share Filing Application for Certificate of Authority	5.00
Total Minimum Fee	$65.00

STATE
WASHINGTON**

Initial fee based on portion of authorized capital stock represented (minimum)	$ 50.00
For Filing Application for Certificate of Authority and Issuing Certificate of Authority	5.00
Annual License Fee (minimum)	30.00
25% Surtax	20.00
Total Minimum Fee	$105.00

WEST VIRGINIA

Issuing Certificate of Authority	$ 10.00
Annual License Tax (prorated)	250.00
Tax on land (5 cents per acre in excess of 10,000 acres)	
Fee to State Auditor for acting as resident attorney (prorated)	10.00
Recording charter and Certificate of Authority (est. minimum)	5.00
Total Minimum Fee	$275.00

WISCONSIN

Filing application for Certificate of Authority (minimum) (Based on capital employed or to be employed)	$50.00

WYOMING

Filing application for and issuing Certificate of Authority In addition there is tax of $1.00 per $1,000.00 in assets.	$10.00

---

* Certified copy of Certificate of Incorporation Required
** Certificate of Good Standing Required
*** A $500 deposit by separate cashier's check is payable to Comptroller of Public Accounts.

Both documents can be obtained directly through a registered agent.

TOTAL APPROXIMATE QUALIFICATION FEES FOR ALL
50 STATES $5,263.55

Either a certified copy of the Certificate of Incorporation (also called (Articles of Incorporation) or certificates of good standing are required in most states. Additional copies of the validated Certificate of Incorporation can be obtained from the Secretary of State's office in Dover, Delaware. Cost is $11.00 for certified copy and $10.00 for certificate of good standing.

(The Company Corporation will supply you with qualification forms for any State at $.50 each for postage and handling.)

As legislation can and does change rapidly, it is advisable to check with the individual State regarding current fee schedules and regulations.

MINIMUM ANNUAL FEE PAYABLE TO CORPORATION DEPARTMENT
FOR FOREIGN AND DOMESTIC CORPORATIONS

SECTION IX—A

STATE	TAX	FOREIGN	DOMESTIC
Ala.	Annual Permit	$5.	$10.
	Franchise Tax	$25.	$25.
Alaska	Annual Corporation Tax	$100.	$50.
	Business License Tax	$25.	$25.
	Renewal of Registered Name	$10.	$10.
Ariz.	Annual Report	$25.	$25.
Ark.	Franchise Tax	$11.	$11.
	(Dom. Corp. organized to do business entirely outside state — $5.)		
	Filing Annual Report		$5.
Calif.	Franchise (Income) Tax	$200.	$200.
Colo.	Annual Franchise Tax	—	$10.
	Annual License Fee	$100.	—
	Annual Report	$5.	$5.
Conn.	Income (Fran.) Tax	$50.	$50.
	License Fee	$100.	(not subject)
	Annual Report	$16.	$16.
Del.	Franchise Tax	(not subject)	$20.
	Annual Report	$30.	$10.
D.C.	Franchise (Income) Tax	$25.	$25.
	Annual Report	$10.	$15
Fla.	Minimum Charter Tax	$30.	$20.
	(Up through 7,500 shares of $1.00 par value or up through 60 shares of no par value)		
	Filing Designation of Agent	$3.	
	Issuing permit to do Business	$15.	$5.
Ga.	Annual License Tax	$10.	$10.
	Annual Report Fee	$5.	$5.
Hawaii	Annual License Fee	$100.	(not subject)
	Annual Corporation Exhibit	$10.	$10.
Ida.	Annual License Tax	$20.	$20.
	Annual Statement	$1.	$1.
Ill.	Franchise Tax	$100.	$100.
	Supplemental Franchise Tax @ 0.5%		
	Annual Report	$15.	$15.
Ind.	Annual Report	$15.	$15.
	Property Tax	—	—

STATE	TAX	FOREIGN	DOMESTIC
Iowa	Annual Corporation Report (Old Law)	(not subject)	$1.
	Annual Report and License Fee (Required under Business Corporation Act of 1959)	$5.	$5.
Kan.	Franchise Tax	$20.	$20.
	Annual Filing of Certificate of Good Standing	—	(not subject)
Ky.	Annual License Fee	$10.	$10.
	Statement of Existence	$4.	(not subject)
	Annual Verification Report	$5.	$5.
	Annual Name Renewal Fee	$12.	(not subject)
La.	Franchise Tax	$10.	$10.
	Filing Annual Report	$5.	$5.
Me.	Filing Fee for Annual Report License Fee	$30.	$30.
Md.	Filing Fee Annual Report	(not subject)	$40.
	Personal Property Return	$40.	(no fee)
Mass.	Corporation Excise Tax	$100.	$100.
	Cert. of Condition Annual Report	$35.	$35.
Mich.	Franchise Tax	$20.	$20.
	Annual Report	$10.	$10.
Minn.	Income Tax	$10.	$10.
	Annual Report	$12.50	(not subject)
Miss.	Franchise Tax	$10.	$10.
	Annual Report	$5.	$5.
Mo.	Franchise Tax	$25.	$25.
	Registration Statement	$5.	$5.
	Anti-Trust Affidavit	$5.	$5.
Mont.	License Tax	$50.	$50.
	Business License Tax	$10.	$10.
	Annual Report	$5.	$5.
Neb.	Corporation "Occupation" tax	$20.	$10.
Nev.	List of Officers, Directors and Agent	$10.	$10.
N.H.	Franchise Tax	(not subject)	$30.
	Annual Maintenance Fee	$70.	(not subject)
	Annual Return	$30.	$30.
N.J.	Net Worth Tax	$50.	$25.
	Annual Report	$15.	$15.
N.M.	Franchise Tax	$10.	$10.
	Annual Report	$5, unless same	($5.)
N.Y	Franchise (Income) Tax	$125.	$125.
N.C.	Franchise Tax	$10.	$10.

STATE	TAX	FOREIGN	DOMESTIC
N.D.	Annual Filing Fee & Taxes	$10.	$20.
Ohio	Franchise Tax	$50.	$50.
Okla.	Franchise Tax	$10.	$10.
	Secretary of State	$40.	—
	Annual Affidavit	$3.	—
Ore.	License Tax	$200.	$10.
	Annual Report	$10.	$10.
Penna.	Capital Stock Tax	$150.	$10.
Puerto Rico	Annual Report	$100.	$100.
	License Fee	$25.	—
R.I.	Annual Franchise Tax	(not subject)	$50.
	Annual Report	$15.	$15.
S.C.	License Tax	$10.	$10.
	Annual Report	$5.	$5.
S.D.	Annual Report	$10.	$10.
Tenn.	Franchise Tax	$10.	$10.
	Annual Report	$25. or $5.	$25. or $5.
		(Depending on basis of Tax, which is left to discretion of corp.)	
Texas	Franchise Tax	$35.	$35.
Utah	Franchise (Income) Tax	$25.	$25.
	Annual Report	$5.	$5.
Vt.	Corporate Income Tax	$50.	$25.
	Annual Report	$25.	$2.
	Application for Renewal of Corporate Name	$25.	(not subject)
Va.	Franchise Tax — Minimum fee on authorized stock ($1 to $50,000 total par value) no par stock deemed to have a par value of $100 per share.	$60.	$20.
	Registration Fee	$10.	$10.
	Annual Report	$5.	$5.
Wash.	License Fee	$30.	$30.
	Annual Report	$2.	$2.
W. Va.	License Tax	$250.	$20.
	Fee to Secretary of State Attorney-in-fact	$10.	$10.
Wisc.	Annual Report	$15.	$7.
Wyo.	License Tax	$5.	$5.

COMMON, PREFERRED, VOTING AND NON-VOTING STOCK

SECTION X

A corporation may issue common or preferred stock with or without par value.

Usually preferred stockholders have priority rights over common stockholders in the event a corporation is liquidated or dissolved. Also, preferred stock usually does not have voting privileges.

Stock in a corporation may also have conditions imposed upon it which permit stockholders either to have or not to have voting privileges. Voting or non-voting stock is usually designated by class, such as class A-voting stock, class B-non-voting stock.

Capital stock can also be issued with a stated value paid for either in cash or by providing services to the corporation. However, under Delaware Corporate Law, no capital is required by a Delaware corporation.

A Delaware corporation may file simple forms with the Secretary of State to add provisions for any of the above types of stock at any time after the corporation is formed.

The forms in this book are directed to a corporation with one class of stock. No par common stock shares (with voting privileges) of up to 1,000 shares are used in the specimen forms. The filing fees both initial and continuing are lowest with this type of format. Also, this kind of approach to the type of stock is simple and serves the needs of most small and medium sized corporations.

On an annual basis, franchise tax is based on the number of authorized shares of stock, irrespective of par value. It's an unnecessary expense to authorize more shares of stock than those necessary to meet the needs of the corporation. On 1,000 shares the annual tax is only $20.00. Examples of fees for more shares are as follows: on i.e. 100,000 shares it is $332.75 and on 1,000,000 shares it is $3,055.25.

If, however, it is desirable to issue other classes of stock initially, this can be easily accomplished by adding language to this effect on the certificate of incorporation, before it is filed with the state.

A registered agent can quote what the state filing fees are for the various types of stock or they may be obtained directly from the Secretary of State, Dover, Delaware.

"NO-PAR" VS. "PAR VALUE" STOCK

SECTION XI

Prior to the 1940's, it was customary for most corporations to issue "par value" stock. This meant that each share had a stated value on its face, such as $3.00, which supposedly represented the amount contributed by the shareholder. However, the value of a share of stock can fluctuate greatly, depending on the overall worth of the corporation, so that the "par value" of the stock becomes misleading and unimportant.

Another type of stock has therefore become increasingly more popular. It is called "no-par value" stock. Under this method, a certificate of stock has no stated value, but merely indicates the number of shares of "no-par value". The actual value would depend on what an investor is willing to pay, and this judgment is based on a number of factors. These factors include the assets owned by the corporation and on assessment by the investors as to the corporation's potential profitability.

In addition, the initial filing fee and annual fees to the State of Delaware are lowest when the corporation issues 1,000 shares or less than $100,000 contributed capital. The minimum filing fee is only $10. The type of stock used as examples in this book is "no-par". "No-par value" stock can be converted to "par value" stock by a corporation merely by filing a simple form with the State of Delaware. This can be forwarded to the Secretary of State by a registered agent including The Company Corporation at a nominal filing fee. On the whole, it's usually simpler and less costly to form a Delaware corporation and qualify it to do business in any state with its shares being no par. At the time of printing there were two exceptions to our knowledge, Florida and Virginia. For these, forming Delaware corporations and qualifying to do business in a home state, it is less costly to originally file the corporation with par value stock.

If a corporation becomes successful and authorizes more shares, as well as acquires substantial assets, there can be substantial annual savings in Delaware Corporate Franchise Taxes by converting the no-par value stock to par value stock.

To raise capital, a corporation can also issue bonds which are usually an interest bearing instrument. A bond is a form of debt financing many corporations prefer over the sale of stock.

In business judgments involving decisions of this type, many times it is desirable to consider ideas of authors, accountants, life insurance advisors, trust officers, lawyers, and other sources of information.

ONLY ONE OFFICER

SECTION XII

The Delaware corporation need only have one person that holds all the company offices. This same individual may act as the incorporator. Likewise, the same person can be the entire board of directors. One officer is the legal minimum.

On the other hand, one can have as many directors, officers or vice presidents as desired. Many corporations find it helpful to invite to its board of directors capable people who may often make substantial contributions in building a successful corporation.

Under a new amendment to Delaware Corporate Law, there is substantially greater flexibility than ever before in many areas, including cutting the number of officers from a minimum of three down to one. Previously, a corporation had to have at least three officers — president, secretary and treasurer. The only requirement now is to have one officer. This enables the corporation to have available a person to sign stock certificates and keep minutes of stockholder and director's meetings when appropriate.

THE CORPORATE NAME

SECTION XIII

The name picked for the new corporation when it is submitted to Delaware will be recorded as long as it is in proper form and as long as no one else is using the same name or one that is too similar, prior to the application of the new corporation. *The name must contain the word association, corporation, club, foundation, fund, company, incorporated, institute, society, union, syndicate, or limited, or one of the abbreviations Co., Corp., Inc., or Ltd.*

Delaware will permit words like the ones above in abbreviated form, provided they are written in Roman characters or letters. Corporate names must be distinguishable on the records of the state from the names of other corporations formed under the laws of Delaware.

A service is provided by the state whereby a corporate name can be reserved for a period of thirty (30) days at no charge. Any person can write the state directly to avail himself of this service. However, it is not necessary that this be done. Registered agents provide this service, usually at low cost.

There are certain property rights under the law which accrue to the original owners of a business name or to a corporation that originates a name. These businesses may legally prevent a new firm from using a name that is the same or similar to theirs. If it is planned that the corporation will qualify as a foreign corporation (see Section VIII) in any state, the corporate name is registered in that state by the act of such a filing. Sometimes a name is available in Delaware but not in another state in which the corporation wishes to qualify. When this occurs the corporate name can easily be changed. Filing cost is $45.00 and $10.00 to Recorder of Deeds for a total of $55.00. Form is available from Secretary of State, Dover, Delaware. Your registered agent can also assist you at a moderate cost.

POTENTIAL PROBLEMS WITH A CORPORATION'S NAME

The effect of a name change varies. Sometimes it just involves new stationery with notification to people with whom the corporation does business. In other cases substantial cost can be incurred, i.e., when a large inventory of packaged goods bear the name. Some businesses use a name change to marketing advantage. Many corporations who have been well established choose to change their name to create a different "image" or to reflect a different line of products or services than existed when the corporation was formed. It is wise to check the yellow pages of the telephone directory when first planning to use a name to see if similar ones exist.

To reduce the possibility of a name change one can contact the Corporation Department in any state to determine if the name is available in advance of filing the form.

When it is known that an existing business uses a certain name, it is prudent not to select a name that is similar to that regardless of where that company is located. Theoretically, a name can be registered in all fifty states to avoid the possibility of a later name change. However, owners of corporations seldom go to this extent. Also an unincorporated business somewhere in the U.S. may be using the same name that the corporation might use and the right to the name could be challenged at some future time. Therefore, unless one were to search every business name in the nation there is always the possibility of a name change at some time during the life of a corporation.

OPERATING ANONYMOUSLY IF DESIRED

SECTION XIV

Many people who are owner(s) of Delaware corporations prefer to remain as anonymous as possible.

In Delaware, a corporation need not disclose who its stockholders are to the Secretary of State. If a person does not wish to disclose who the officer(s) and/or director(s) are, there are three ways this can be accomplished.

The first method is by having an acquaintance, friend or relative of the founder(s) hold all the company offices. This person does not have to be a stockholder in the corporation. (This person, however, should be advised that he could be liable in the event of a tax delinquency or for any illegal action by the founder.)

The second way is to obtain and register a legal fictitious name (many authors use this approach commonly called a "pen" name). A fictitious name can be registered in a Prothonotary's office in Delaware for $1.00. Other states have a similar procedure. Then this name can be used for corporate purposes and to sign checks, etc. Registering a fictitious name can be accomplished where you reside at the Recorder of Deeds or Prothonotary's office (or its equivalent, county clerk, etc.) or in Delaware.

The third method is by the corporation not filing the annual report to the Secretary of State's office. This report is a simple form that is completed once each year. It basically indicates who the corporation's officers are, how many shares of stock have been authorized, and other data on the corporation's assets. It lists officer(s), director(s) and number of shares. The state imposes a $25 annual fine to corporations who do not file this report. Many Delaware corporations have in the past years elected to pay this annual fine rather than file the report, although the state frowns on this practice.

The first and second methods are simpler and less costly, and therefore, are recommended over the third for persons who wish to operate the corporation anonymously.

DEDUCTION OF CORPORATE STOCK LOSS FROM PERSONAL INCOME

SECTION XV

A valuable tax law exists that is beneficial to shareholders of a corporation.

Internal Revenue Code, Section 1244, enables a shareholder to deduct certain losses in investment of stock as ordinary income losses. Experienced tax lawyers sometimes advise their clients of the existence of this tax law.

Under Section 1244 and subject to its conditions, should a shareholder in a corporation (shareholder can be any individual, but not a corporation, estate or trust) incur any kind of loss through sale of his stock at a loss or if the stock becomes worthless, this section enables a deduction of the loss up to $50,000 a year ($100,000 on a joint return) from personal income. Normally a loss on a stock investment is not deductible and is subject to special "capital loss limitations" under the Internal Revenue Code. Shareholders have nothing to lose, since there are no disadvantages of qualifying the corporation under this tax provision if the corporation is eligible, as most small ones are. The potential tax benefits are well worth it. Also, more investors are potentially attracted toward the purchase of stock in the corporation when the person is made aware of this provision. Of course, a person should always be cautious in how and to whom stock in a corporation is offered so that the Federal Securities regulations under the Securities Act of 1933 are not violated.

What must be done is to merely arrange to have this legal principle put into effect upon the formation of the corporation by completing simple forms. Nothing has to be filed with the Internal Revenue Service. A copy of the Internal Revenue Section 1244 is on the following page. One registered agent service company, The Company Corporation, provides standard forms to all clients as a standard part of their service. (See Section VII)

NOTE: Every "Sub-Chapter S" corporation (See Section XVI) should qualify under Section 1244. "Sub-Chapter S" and Section 1244 complement each other in the tax advantages they provide. Operating losses of a "Sub-Chapter S" corporation may be passed on to the stockholders currently; a loss in value in the assets of a Section 1244 corporation can be taken as an "ordinary loss" on the sale and exchange of stock.

LOSSES ON SMALL BUSINESS STOCK

SECTION 1244 I.R.C. OF 1954

(a) GENERAL RULE — In the case of an individual, a loss on Section 1244 stock issued to such individual or to a partnership which would (but for this section) be treated as a loss from the sale or exchange of a capital asset shall, to the extent provided in this section, be treated as a loss from the sale or exchange of an asset which is not a capital asset.

(b) MAXIMUM AMOUNT FOR ANY TAXABLE YEAR — For any taxable year the aggregate amount treated by the taxpayer by reason of this section as a loss from the sale or exchange of an asset which is not a capital asset shall not exceed —

(1) $50,000, or

(2) $100,000, in the case of a husband and wife filing a joint return for such year under section 6013.

(c) SECTION 1244 STOCK DEFINED —

(1) IN GENERAL — For purposes of this section, the term "section 1244 stock" means common stock in a domestic corporation if —

(A) such corporation adopted a plan after June 30, 1958, to offer such stock for a period (ending not later than two years after the date such plan was adopted) specified in the plan,

(B) at the time such plan was adopted, such corporation was a small business corporation,

(C) at the time such plan was adopted, no portion of a prior offering was outstanding,

(D) such stock was issued by such corporation, pursuant to such plan, for money or other property (other than stock and securities), and

(E) such corporation, during the period of its 5 most recent taxable years ending before the date the loss on such stock is sustained (or if such corporation has not been in existence for 5 taxable years ending before such date, during the period of its taxable years ending before such date; or if such corporation has not been in existence for one taxable year ending before such date, during the period such corporation has been in existence before such date), derived more than 50 percent of its aggregate gross receipts from sources other than royalties, rents, dividends, interest, annuities; and sales or exchanges of stock or securities (gross receipts from such sales or exchanges being taken into account for purposes of this subparagraph only to the extent of gains therefrom); except that this subparagraph shall not apply with respect to any corporation if, for the period referred to, the amount of the deductions allowed by this chapter (other than by sections 172, 242, 243, 244, and 245) exceed the amount of gross income.

Such term does not include stock if issued (pursuant to the plan referred to in subparagraph (A)) after a subsequent offering of stock has been made by the corporation.

(2) SMALL BUSINESS CORPORATION DEFINED — For purposes of this section, a corporation shall be treated as a small business corporation if at the time of the adoption of the plan —

(A) the sum of —

    (i)   the aggregate amount which may be offered under the plan, plus

    (ii)   the aggregate amount of money and other property (taken into account in an amount, as of the time received by the corporation, equal to the adjusted basis to the corporation of such property for determining gain, reduced by any liabilities to which the property was subject or which were assumed by the corporation at such time) received by the corporation after June 30, 1958, for stock, as a contribution to capital, and as paid-in surplus,

does not exceed $500,000; and

(B) the sum of —

    (i)   the aggregate amount which may be offered under the plan, plus

    (ii)   the equity capital of the corporation (determined on the date of the adoption of the plan),

does not exceed $1,000,000.

For purposes of subparagraph (B), the equity capital of a corporation is the sum of its money and other property (in an amount equal to the adjusted basis of such property for determining gain), less the amount of its indebtedness (other than indebtedness to shareholders).

(d) SPECIAL RULES —

(1) LIMITATIONS ON AMOUNT OF ORDINARY LOSS —

(A) CONTRIBUTIONS OF PROPERTY HAVING BASIS IN EXCESS OF VALUE — If —

    (i)   section 1244 stock was issued in exchange for property,

    (ii)   the basis of such stock in the hands of the taxpayer is determined by reference to the basis in his hands of such property, and

    (iii)   the adjusted basis (for determining loss) of such property immediately before the exchange exceeded its fair market value at such time.

then in computing the amount of the loss on such stock for purposes of this section the basis of such stock shall be reduced by an amount equal to the excess described in clause (iii).

(B) INCREASES IN BASIS — In computing the amount of the loss on stock for purposes of this section, any increase in the basis of such stock (through contributions to the capital of the corporation, or otherwise) shall be treated as allocable to stock which is not section 1244 stock.

(2) RECAPITALIZATIONS, CHANGES IN NAME, ETC. — To the extent provided in regulations prescribed by the Secretary or his delegate, common stock in a corporation, the basis of which (in the hands of a taxpayer) is determined in whole or in part by reference to the basis in his hands of stock in such corporation which meets the requirements of subsection (c) (1) (other than subparagraph (E) thereof), or which is received in a reorganization described in section 368(a) (1) (F) in exchange for stock which meets such requirements, shall be treated as meeting such requirements. For purposes of paragraphs (1) (E) and (2) (A) subsection (c), a successor corporation in a reorganization described in section 368(a) (1) (F) shall be treated as the same corporation as its predecessor.

(3) RELATIONSHIP TO NET OPERATING LOSS DEDUCTION — For purposes of section 172 (relating to the net operating loss deduction), any amount of loss treated by reason of this section as a loss from the sale or exchange of an asset which is not a capital asset shall be treated as attributable to a trade or business of the taxpayer.

(4) INDIVIDUAL DEFINED — For purposes of this section, the term "individual" does not include a trust or estate.

(e) REGULATIONS — The Secretary or his delegate shall prescribe such regulations as may be necessary to carry out the purposes of this section.

BENEFITS OF CORPORATIONS TAXED AS A
PROPRIETORSHIP OR PARTNERSHIP

SECTION XVI

A corporation has the tax option of either having its profits taxed under corporation tax rates or under individual income tax rates. Tax rates on corporate income are listed on page 5. If the corporation pays dividends, tax must be paid on them.

The Internal Revenue Code permits a corporation's profits to be taxed *individually* to the owner(s). The code refers to this type of corporation as a "small business corporation" or Sub-Chapter "S" corporation.

In some individual cases, as in closely held corporations, a person's taxes would be less if taxed as an individual. Under the Internal Revenue Code, therefore, provisions are made so that a person can legally have all the advantages of a corporation and still have the option to be taxed either as a corporation or as an individual.

Under "Sub-Chapter S", a profitable corporation can avoid double taxation. A very profitable corporation pays taxes on profits. Another tax is paid by its stockholders if the corporation pays dividends. "Sub-Chapter S" taxes on profits or deductions on losses are at *individual rates.* "Sub-Chapter S" taxation applies to stockholders who own 5% or more of a corporation.

A person can call any Internal Revenue office and obtain Form 2553. This is a one page form which permits tax filing as a small business corporation. Corporations eligible to elect small business corporation tax status must meet five simple requirements. The following is a quotation from Form 2553: "Corporations eligible to elect. — The election may be made only if the corporation is a domestic* corporation which meets all five of the following requirements:

1. It has no more than fifteen shareholders; however, if stock is held by husband and wife as joint tenants, tenants by the entirety, or tenants in common, or is community property (or the income from which is community income) it shall be treated as owned by one shareholder.

2. It has only individuals or estates as shareholders.

3. It has no shareholder who is a non-resident alien.

4. It has only one class of stock.

5. It is not a member of an affiliated group of corporations as defined in Section 1504 of the Code."

A copy of Form 2553 is on the following page.

The type of tax return a person completes if he elects to be taxed under Sub-Chapter "S" is Form 1120S. Internal Revenue offices have instructions for filing Form 1120S, which can be obtained at no charge by calling their office. This form can be completed without professional help. However, any good accountant can assist in completing this form if desired. (Do not send tax forms to your registered agent.)

* Any corporation anywhere in the United States.

46

Form **2553**

Department of the Treasury
Internal Revenue Service

Election by a Small Business Corporation

(As to taxable status under subchapter S of the Internal Revenue Code)

Note: This election under section 1372(a) (with the consent of all your shareholders) to be treated as an "electing small business corporation" for income tax purposes may be made only if the corporation meets all six of the requirements stated in instruction A. See section 1372(e) which describes certain conditions whereby the status of an electing small business corporation may be revoked or terminated.

Name of corporation	Employer identification number (see Instruction L)	Principal business activity and specific product or service (see Instruction F)
Number and street		Election is to be effective for the taxable year beginning (Month, day, year)
City or town, State and ZIP code		Number of shares issued and outstanding (see Instruction E)

Is the corporation the outgrowth or continuation of any form of predecessor? . . . ☐ Yes ☐ No | Date and place of incorporation

If "Yes," state name of predecessor, type of organization, and period during which it was in existence ▶ ....

If this election is effective for the first taxable year the corporation is in existence, complete A through H below, otherwise complete E through H.

A Date corporation first had shareholders	B Date corporation first had assets	C Date corporation began doing business	D Annual return will be filed for taxable year ending (month)

E Name and address (including ZIP code) of each shareholder	F Shareholders' Statement of Consent. We the undersigned shareholders consent to the election of the above corporation to be treated as an "electing small business corporation" under section 1372(a). (Signature of shareholders and date)	G Stock owned		H Social Security number
		Number of shares	Dates acquired	
1				
2				
3				
4				
5				
6				
7				
8				
9				
10				
11				
12				
13				
14				
15				

Note: For this election to be valid, the consent of each shareholder must be shown above, or the consent of each shareholder must be attached to this form. (See instruction D.)

Under penalties of perjury, I declare that I have examined this election, including accompanying schedules and statements, and to the best of my knowledge and belief it is true, correct, and complete.

Signature and
Title of Officer ▶ _____   Date ▶ _____

Purpose

(References are to the Internal Revenue Code.)

The purpose of this election is to permit the undistributed taxable income of an "electing small business corporation" to be taxed to the shareholders rather than the corporation. The term "undistributed taxable income" means taxable income (as computed under section 1373(d)) minus the sum of (1) the tax imposed by sections 56 and 1378(a) and (2) the amount of money distributed as dividends out of earnings and profits of the taxable year.

Instructions

A. Corporations eligible to elect.—The corporation may make the election only if it meets all six of the following requirements:

1. it is a domestic corporation
2. it has no more than 15 shareholders

   Note: *For purposes of requirement 2 above, a husband and wife (and their estates) shall be treated as one shareholder.*

3. it has only individuals, estates, or certain trusts as shareholders
4. it has no nonresident alien shareholders
5. it has only one class of stock
6. it is not a member of an affiliated group of corporations (as defined in section 1504).

   Note: *A corporation is not considered a member of an affiliated group if it owns stock in a corporation that has not begun business before the close of the taxable year to which the election applies and does not have taxable income during that year.*

B. When to make the election.

1. For taxable years beginning after December 31, 1978, complete Form 2553 and file it either (1) any time during the preceding taxable year, or (2) any time during the first 75 days of the tax year. If an election is made after the first 75 days of the tax year and on or before the last day of such tax year, such election shall be treated as made for the following tax year.

2. For taxable years beginning before January 1, 1979, Form 2553 was required to be filed either (1) during the first month of that year, or (2) during the month before the first month. For example, a 1978 calendar year corporation must have made the election either in January 1978 or in December 1977 for the election to be effective for the 1978 tax year.

A prior year election which was not timely filed may be corrected if certain conditions are met. See section 5(d) of Public Law 95–628 for details concerning a perfecting election.

For purposes of this election, a new corporation's taxable year begins when it has shareholders, acquires assets, or begins doing business, whichever happens first. (See regulation 1.1372–2(b) for other details.)

The election will be effective for the taxable year for which it is made and for all later years unless it is terminated or revoked under section 1372(e).

C. Valid election.—The election will be valid only if all persons who are shareholders in such corporation on the day on which such election is made consent to such election.

D. Shareholder's statement of consent.—On the date of election, each shareholder must consent to the election either by signing the Shareholders' Statement of Consent (item F on Form 2553) or by signing a separate statement which must be attached to Form 2553 and must include:

1. the name and address of the corporation and of the shareholder,

2. the number of shares of stock owned by the shareholder,
3. the dates the shares were acquired, and
4. a statement that the shareholder consents to the corporation's election to be treated as a small business corporation under section 1372(a).

If you wish, you may incorporate the consents of all shareholders in one statement.

The consent must be signed by both husband and wife if they have a community interest in the stock or the income from it, and by each tenant in common, each joint tenant, and each tenant by the entirety.

The consent of a minor shall be made by the minor or the minor's legal guardian, or the minor's natural guardian if no legal guardian has been appointed (even in the case of stock held by a custodian for a minor under a statute patterned after the Uniform Gifts to Minors Act).

New Shareholder.—An election by a small business corporation shall terminate if a new shareholder (any person who was not a shareholder on the day on which the election was made) becomes a shareholder in such corporation and affirmatively refuses to consent to the election on or before the 60th day after the day on which the new shareholder acquires the stock.

The new shareholder's affirmative refusal to consent to the election must be filed with the Internal Revenue Service Center having jurisdiction for the area in which the principal business, office or agency of the corporation is located.

If the new shareholder is the estate of a decedent, the 60-day period for affirmatively refusing to consent to the election shall expire on the 60th day after (1) the day on which the executor or administrator of the estate qualifies, or (2) the last day of the taxable year of the corporation in which the decedent died, whichever is earlier.

Any termination of an election by reason of the affirmative refusal of any person to consent to such election shall be effective for the taxable year of the corporation in which such person becomes a shareholder (or if later, the first taxable year for which such election would otherwise have been effective) and for all succeeding taxable years of the corporation. (See section 1372(e)(1).)

E. Number of shares issued and outstanding.—This block should contain only one figure for stock both issued and outstanding. This figure will be the number of shares of stock that have been issued to shareholders and have not been reacquired by the corporation. This number must equal the total number of shares owned by all shareholders as reported in item G of Form 2553.

F. Principal business activity and principal product or service.—In reporting the principal business activity give the one business activity that accounts for the largest percentage of "total receipts." "Total receipts" means gross sales and gross receipts, plus all other income. State the principal product or service as well as the principal business activity. For example, if the principal business activity is "Grain mill products," the principal product or service may be "cereal preparation." See Codes for Principal Business Activity at the back of the Instructions for Form 1120S, U.S. Small Business Corporation Income Tax Return.

G. Where to file.—File this election with the Internal Revenue Service Center where the corporation will file Form 1120S, U.S. Small Business Corporation Income Tax Return. A copy should also be retained for the permanent files of the corporation.

If the corporation's principal business, office or agency is located in	Use the following Internal Revenue Service Center address
New Jersey, New York City and counties of Nassau, Rockland, Suffolk, and Westchester	Holtsville, NY 00501
New York (all other counties), Connecticut, Maine, Massachusetts, New Hampshire, Rhode Island, Vermont	Andover, MA 05501
Alabama, Florida, Georgia, Mississippi, South Carolina	Atlanta, GA 31101
Michigan, Ohio	Cincinnati, OH 45999
Arkansas, Kansas, Louisiana, New Mexico, Oklahoma, Texas	Austin, TX 73301
Alaska, Arizona, Colorado, Idaho, Minnesota, Montana, Nebraska, Nevada, North Dakota, Oregon, South Dakota, Utah, Washington, Wyoming	Ogden, UT 84201
Illinois, Iowa, Missouri, Wisconsin	Kansas City, MO 64999
California, Hawaii	Fresno, CA 93888
Indiana, Kentucky, North Carolina, Tennessee, Virginia, West Virginia	Memphis, IN 37501
Delaware, District of Columbia, Maryland, Pennsylvania	Philadelphia, PA 19255

H. Signature.—This form must be signed by the president, vice president, treasurer, assistant treasurer, chief accounting officer, or any other corporate officer (such as tax officer) who is authorized to sign.

I. Election after termination or revocation.—If an election has been terminated or revoked under section 1372(e), see section 1372(f) and section 1.1372–5 of the regulations for the restrictions on eligibility to make a new election.

J. Investment credit property.—Section 47 and the regulations thereunder provide that investment credit property ceases to be investment credit property when a corporation makes a valid election under section 1372 to be an "electing small business corporation" and the tax recomputation provisions of section 47 will apply.

The corporation and its shareholders may, however, execute the agreement specified in section 1.47–4(b)(2) of the regulations so that the recapture provisions of section 1.47–1(a) of the regulations will not apply to the section 38 property.

K. Work incentive (WIN) program credit.—Section 1.50A–5(b)(1) of the regulations provides that certain WIN wages paid prior to January 1, 1979, for which the WIN credit was claimed will cease to qualify as WIN wages when a corporation makes a valid election under section 1372 to be an "electing small business corporation." Therefore, the recapture provisions of section 1.50A–3 of the regulations may apply. However, the corporation and its shareholders may execute the agreement specified in section 1.50A–5(b)(2) of the regulations so that the recapture provisions of section 1.50A–3 of the regulations will not apply to the WIN expenses because of the corporation's election under section 1372.

L. Employer identification number.—Corporations that have not applied for an employer identification number should enter "not applied for." If a number has been applied for but not received, enter "applied for."

Corporations which do not have an EIN should apply for one on Form SS–4, available from any IRS or Social Security Administration office. Send Form SS–4 to the same Internal Revenue Service Center to which Form 1120S is sent.

NONPROFIT CORPORATIONS

SECTION XVII

A nonprofit corporation is a special type of corporation formed for charitable and other purposes that are not profit seeking. It has many of the features of standard corporations with the major exception being its tax status.

The number of nonprofit corporations in the United States is remarkable, running into the hundreds of thousands. In some states like Ohio and New York, over one-third of all corporations chartered there are nonprofit. While there are critics of the growing phenomenon of the nonprofit corporation, in some towns and cities over 50% of the property is tax exempt. However, as long as the minimal requirements of IRS are met, it is legal under existing law and it is likely to keep expanding and growing.

Nonprofit corporations do not issue stock. Instead membership certificates are often used. The form for a nonstock, nonprofit corporation that is recommended for use is on the following page. It can be completed in the same way as the earlier certificates in this book and either mailed directly to the Secretary of State or through a registered agent.

Some individuals utilize nonprofit corporations as a tax shelter. Many corporate situations lend themselves to this tax exempt status. These endeavors can provide desirable tax advantages to the owner(s) of a corporation that may qualify for a government grant, to do research, educational experiments, etc.

A corporation can often qualify for tax exempt status and still pay its officers salaries and expenses. The salary and expenses may be questioned by the Internal Revenue Service on a tax audit if it is "excessive".

Other situations lending themselves to a nonprofit status are religious, fraternal and civic clubs. Also neighborhood associations often incorporate as a nonprofit corporation primarily to gain personal liability protection for its members.

Still another is when a person or group of persons create a nonprofit foundation for variants of charitable purposes such as for medical research.

Often a person's will can be worded so as to leave such assets as a list of stockholdings, insurance proceeds (by insurance contract) to a nonprofit corporation that was organized by that person while still alive.

Since personal contributions to many nonprofit corporations are tax deductible, many tax exempt corporations utilize this incentive to obtain substantial funds often running into the millions of dollars for its operations. There are many fund raising firms that have organized to help nonprofit corporations with fund raising.

Owners of a nonprofit corporation should contact an Internal Revenue office and obtain forms to qualify for tax exempt status. See IRS booklet No. 557.

CERTIFICATE OF INCORPORATION
of
Association of Sunshine

FIRST: The name of this corporation is _____ Association of Sunshine _____
(exactly as in heading)

SECOND: Its registered office in the State of Delaware is to be located at 1300 Market Street in the City of Wilmington, County of New Castle. The registered agent in charge thereof is The Company Corporation at same address.

THIRD: The nature of the business and the objects and purposes proposed to be transacted, promoted and carried on, are to do any or all the things herein mentioned, as fully and to the same extent as natural persons might or could do, and in any part of the world, viz:

The purpose of the corporation is to engage in any lawful act or activity for which corporations may be organized under the general Corporation Law of Delaware.

(See IRS circular number 557 available at any IRS office for guidance in completing this blank)

FOURTH: The corporation shall not have any capital stock and the conditions of membership shall be stated in By-Laws.

FIFTH: The name and mailing address of the incorporator is as follows: _____
(Leave blank if using The Company Corporation, otherwise your name and address)

SIXTH: The powers of the incorporator are to terminate upon filing of the certificate of incorporation, and the name(s) and mailing address(es) of the persons who are to serve as director(s) until their successors are elected are as follows:
Frank Moonlight, 1 Park Ave., New York, N.Y.

SEVENTH: The activities and affairs of the corporation shall be managed by a board of directors. The number of directors which shall constitute the whole board shall be such as from time to time shall be fixed by or in the manner provided in, the By-Laws, but in no case shall the number be less than one. The directors need not be members of the corporation unless so required by the By-Laws. The board of directors shall be elected by the members at the annual meeting of the corporation to be held on such date as the By-Laws may provide, and shall hold office until their successors are respectively elected and qualified. The By-Laws shall specify the number of directors necessary to constitute a quorum. The board of directors may, by resolution or resolutions, passed by a majority of the whole board, designate one or more committees which, to the extent provided in said resolution or resolutions or in the By-Laws of the corporation, shall have and may exercise all the powers of the board of directors in the management of the activities and affairs of the corporation and may have power to authorize the seal of the corporation to be affixed to all papers which may require it; and such committee or committees shall have such name or names as may be stated in the By-Laws of the corporation or as may be determined from time to time by resolution adopted by the board of directors. The directors of the corporation may, if the By-Laws so provide, be classified as to term of office. The corporation may elect such officers as the By-Laws may specify, who shall, subject to the provision of the Statute, have titles and exercise such duties as the By-Laws may provide. The board of directors is expressly authorized to make, alter or repeal the By-Laws of this corporation. This corporation may in its By-Laws confer powers upon its board of directors in addition to the foregoing, and in addition to the powers and authorities expressly conferred upon them by the Statute, provided that the board of directors shall not exercise any power of authority conferred herein or by Statute upon the members.

EIGHTH: Meetings of members may be held without the State of Delaware, if the By-Laws so provide. The books of the corporation may be kept (subject to any provision contained in the Statutes) outside the State of Delaware at such place or places as may be from time to time designated by the board of directors.

51

NINTH: No part of the net earnings of the corporation shall inure to the benefit of, or be distributable to, its members, directors, officers or other private persons, except that the corporation shall be authorized and empowered to pay reasonable compensation for services rendered and to make payments and distributions in furtherance of the purposes set forth in Article Third hereof. No substantial part of the activities of the corporation shall be the carrying on of propaganda, or otherwise attempting to intervene in (including the publishing or distribution of statements) any political campaign on behalf of any candidate for public office. Notwithstanding any other provision of these articles, the corporatin shall not carry on any other activities not permitted to be carried on (a) by a corporation exempt from Federal income tax under section 501 (c)(3) of the Internal Revenue Code of 1954 (or the corresponding provision of any future United States Internal Revenue Law) or (b) by a corporation, contributions to which are deductible under section 170 (c)(2) of the Internal Revenue Code of 1954 (or the corresponding provision of any future United States Internal Revenue Law).

TENTH: Upon the dissolution of the corporation, the Board of Directors shall, after paying or making provision for the payment of all of the liabilities of the corporation, dispose of all of the assets of the corporation exclusively for the purposes of the corporation in such manner, or to such organization or organizations organized and operated exclusively for charitable, educational, religious, or scientific purposes as shall at the time qualify as an exempt organization or organizations under section 501 (c)(3) of the Internal Revenue Code of 1954 (or the corresponding provision of any future United States Law) as the Board of Directors shall determine. Any such assets not so disposed of shall be disposed of by the Court of Common Pleas of the county in which the principal office of the corporation is then located, exclusively for such purposes or to such organization or organizations, as said Court shall determine, which are organized and operated exclusively for such purposes.

ELEVENTH: The corporation reserves the right to amend, alter, change or repeal any provision contained in this certificate of incorporation, in the manner now or hereafter prescribed by the Statute, and all rights conferred upon members herein are granted subject to this reservation.

I, THE UNDERSIGNED, being each of the incorporator hereinbefore named, for the purpose of forming a corporation pursuant to Chapter 1 of Title 8 of the Delaware Code, do make this certificate, hereby declaring and certifying that the facts herein stated are true, and accordingly have hereunto set my hand this _____ day of _____ , A.D. 19_____ .

_____

PROFESSIONAL CORPORATIONS

SECTION XVIII

Professionals in some of the United States may be able to take advantage of the benefits of Delaware Corporate Laws.

The same form as for a business corporation is usable by a professional. Professionals should add the initials "P.A." (Professional Association) or "P.C." (Professional Corporation) to the corporate title on the certificate of incorporation, i.e., Jones & Smith, (P.A.). The words Inc., etc., do not appear.

However, professionals* such as doctors, dentists, architects, lawyers, etc. are treated differently under the law than are business corporations due to the nature of the professional's activities (the term "professional" here relates to a person providing a service for which a license is required).

In order to assure that the corporation status for the professional is not disallowed for tax purposes, the corporation that is engaged in the business of providing professional service must —

A. Be owned by professionals of the same field and within the same professional practice (within the same office).

B. Make provisions by agreement to leave stock to other professionals in the same profession and within the same practice and have a purchase agreement in the event of death with the same provisions.

C. Not engage in any other business or activity with a professional in the same practice or investment of any kind other than that of providing the primary professional service such as dentistry, etc.

D. Make certain that the professional relationship between the person furnishing the professional service and the person receiving it does not eliminate the personal liability of the professional for misconduct or negligence.

NOTE: Since the corporate laws from state to state vary greatly with regard to professionals, it is advisable to write the Secretary of State in the state where the professional practices to obtain any other provisions that should be included in the records of this type of Delaware corporation.

Some states have licensing requirements *that do not permit* (particularly physicians) a professional corporation to be formed *out of state*; so that a Delaware professional corporation is only possible for professionals licensed in Delaware. In order to be completely safe, a professional should request an opinion in writing of the *licensing* department of that state *before* proceeding with the formation of a Delaware corporation.

---

*   More detailed information on this subject, covering all 50 states, and containing tear-out forms, can be found in HOW TO FORM YOUR OWN PROFESSIONAL CORPORATION by Ted Nicholas, Enterprise Publishing Company, Two West Eighth Street, Wilmington, Delaware 19801.

FOR ADDITIONAL INFORMATION

SECTION XIX

To obtain a complete copy of the Delaware Corporation Law, write to The Company Corporation, Corporation Center, 725 Market Street, Wilmington, Delaware 19801, and send $3.95 plus $.45 postage and handling. This publication completely outlines the entire corporation law. The writing is cumbersome. Nevertheless, it is well indexed and gives various kinds of helpful information.

If a reader wishes to make an interesting comparison between the advantages of Delaware Corporation Laws versus those of any other state, he may write the Secretary of State, c/o Corporation Department of any state and request information on obtaining a copy of the corporation laws.

CORPORATIONS FORMED IN STATES OTHER THAN DELAWARE

SECTION XX

A corporation in existence and formed in any state other than Delaware may wish to register to do business in Delaware.

On the next page is a specimen Foreign Corporation Certificate. An official of the "foreign" corporation (foreign to Delaware) may complete the form. A Registered Agent in Delaware must be appointed. (The Company Corporation will forward the form to the Secretary of State and act as Registered Agent for an initial annual fee of $25.) The Registered Agent then files the form with the Secretary of State, Dover, Delaware. The State Tax and fees covering the registration of a "foreign" corporation is $85.00. This approach applies best when a non-Delaware corporation wants to register to do business in Delaware. However, there is an approach to obtaining all the benefits of Delaware Corporate Law which the above does not accomplish. This method is favored by more and more corporations. This includes large corporations as well as one-man or family corporations. The objective to the following approach here is to arrange for an existing corporation to obtain the advantages of Delaware Corporate Laws.

A new Delaware corporation is formed and the non-Delaware corporation (i.e., a New York corporation) is merged into the new Delaware corporation. The Delaware fee for a merger is approximately $55.00, if both corporations have simple formats and no more stock is issued by the surviving Delaware corporation.

An agreement is made between the corporations that outlines the terms of the merger between the corporations which includes how many shares of the old corporation for how many shares of the new corporation is helpful. This agreement becomes part of the new corporation's records. After the agreement is completed, a Registered Agent can assist in filing the forms with the state.

To take advantage of Delaware Law, in almost all cases it pays to form a new Delaware corporation and merge the old one into the new one.

FOREIGN CORPORATION CERTIFICATE

THE UNDERSIGNED, a corporation duly organized and existing under the laws of the State of _____ , in accordance with the provisions of Section 371 of Title 8 of the Delaware Code, does hereby certify:

FIRST: That
is a corporation duly organized and existing under the laws of the State of and is filing herewith a certificate evidencing its corporate existence.

SECOND: That the name and address of its registered agent in said State of Delaware upon whom service of process may be had is

THIRD: That the assets of said corporation are $ and that the liabilities thereof are $. The assets and liabilities indicated are as of a date within six months prior to the filing date of this certificate.

FOURTH: That the business which it proposes to do in the State of Delaware is as follows:

FIFTH: That the business which it proposes to do in the State of Delaware is a business it is authorized to do in the Jurisdiction of its Incorporation.

IN WITNESS WHEREOF, said Corporation has caused this Certificate to be signed on its behalf and its corporate seal affixed this day of   , 19

(CORPORATE SEAL)   _____

_____
President

**MINUTES, BY-LAWS, ARTICLES OF INCORPORATION
STANDARD FORMS, REVIEW**

SECTION XXI

On the following pages are specimens of all the forms necessary for a new corporation to have.

A review of the procedure in forming a Delaware corporation without the services of a registered agent is:

1. Arrange to obtain Delaware street mailing address, if practical.

2. File certificate of incorporation with the Secretary of State in Dover, Delaware.

3. When the Certificate is returned from the Secretary of State, file a copy with the Recorder of Deeds office using the Delaware mailing address.

4. Prepare forms based on specimens in this book or order from The Company Corporation.

5. Fill in the blanks on those forms with appropriate information. Keep these forms with the corporate records. From time to time, keep a record of any meeting the Director(s) has by using these forms and filling in the blanks.

6. If desirable, buy stock certificates (either printed or unprinted) from a stationery store.

7. Purchase a corporate seal. This can also be purchased at a stationery store.

The following is a list of the included specimen forms* in this section of book:

A. Statement of Incorporator in lieu of Organization Meeting. This form may be used in all cases and all types of Corporations. Signature(s) same as appear on Certificate of Incorporation.

B. First meeting of Directors. Complete and use only if there is more than one director. This form does not need to be used if the corporation is a close corporation.

C. Waiver of Notice. Complete and use only if there is more than one director.

D. Organization Meeting Form. Complete and use only if there is no more than one director. One person holds all offices. This form does not need to be used if the corporation is a close corporation.

E. By-Laws and Articles of Incorporation. Complete and use in all cases and keep with the corporate records.

NOTE: *Do not send any of the following forms to your registered agent. They are to be kept with your corporate records.*

* Forms reprinted with permission of Excelsior-Legal Stationery Co., Inc.

STATEMENT BY INCORPORATOR(S) OF ACTION TAKEN
IN LIEU OF ORGANIZATION MEETING OF

_____

The undersigned being the incorporator(s) of the corporation make the following statement of action taken to organize the corporation in lieu of an organization meeting.

By-laws regulating the conduct of the business and affairs of the corporation were adopted and appended to this statement.

The following person(s) were appointed director(s) of the corporation until the first annual meeting of the stockholders or until their successors shall be elected or appointed and shall qualify:

The director(s) were authorized and directed to issue from time to time the shares of capital stock of the corporation, now or hereafter authorized, wholly or partly for cash, or labor done, or services performed, or for personal property, or real property or leases thereof, received for the use and lawful purposes of the corporation, or for any consideration permitted by law, as in the discretion of the director(s) may seem for the best interests of the corporation.

_____

_____

_____

The following are to be appended to this statement:

Copy of the Certificate of Incorporation
By-Laws

58

The STATEMENT BY INCORPORATOR(S) OF ACTION TAKEN IN LIEU OF ORGANIZATION MEETING, together with a copy of the By-laws which were adopted in said statement, was then presented to the meeting by the secretary.

Thereupon, on motion duly made, seconded and unanimously carried, it was

RESOLVED, that the STATEMENT BY INCORPORATOR(S) OF ACTION TAKEN IN LIEU OF ORGANIZATION MEETING, dated   19 which has been presented to this meeting, be and hereby is in all respects approved, ratified and confirmed and further

RESOLVED, that the By-laws in the form adopted by the incorporator(s) in the aforementioned statement be and hereby are adopted as and for the By-laws of this corporation.

The secretary then presented and read to the meeting a copy of the certificate of incorporation of the corporation and reported that on the day of   19 the original thereof was duly filed in the office of the Secretary of State and that a certified copy thereof was recorded on   19   in the office of the Recorder of the County of

Upon motion duly made, seconded and carried said report was adopted and the secretary was directed to append to these minutes a certified copy of the certificate of incorporation.

The chairman presented and read, article by article, the proposed by-laws for the conduct and regulation of the business and affairs of the corporation.

Upon motion duly made, seconded and carried, they were adopted and in all respects, ratified, confirmed and approved, as and for the By-laws of the corporation. The secretary was directed to cause them to be inserted in the minute book.

The secretary submitted to the meeting a seal proposed for use as the corporate seal of the corporation. Upon motion duly made, seconded and carried; it was

RESOLVED, that the seal now presented at this meeting, an impression of which is directed to be made in the margin of the minute book, be and the same hereby is adopted as the seal of the corporation.

The chairman then suggested that the secretary of the corporation be authorized to procure the necessary books and that the treasurer of the corporation be authorized to pay all expenses and to reimburse all persons for expenses made in connection with the organization of this corporation. After discussion, on motion duly made, seconded and unanimously carried, it was

RESOLVED, that the secretary of this corporation be and he hereby is authorized and directed to procure all corporate books, books of account and share certificate books required by the statutes of the State of Delaware or necessary or appropriate in connection with the business of this corporation; and it was further

RESOLVED, that the treasurer of this corporation be and he hereby is authorized to pay all charges and expenses incident to or arising out of the organization of this corporation and to reimburse any person who has made any disbursements therefor.

The secretary then presented to the meeting a proposed form of certificates for fully paid and non-assessable shares of stock of this corporation. The chairman directed that the specimen copy of such form of certificate be annexed to the minutes of the meeting. Upon motion duly made, seconded and unanimously carried it was;

RESOLVED, that the form of certificate for fully paid and non-assessable shares of stock of this corporation submitted to this meeting, be and it hereby is adopted as the certificate to represent fully paid and non-assessable shares of stock and that a specimen of such certificate be annexed to the minutes of the meeting.

MINUTES OF THE FIRST MEETING OF
THE BOARD OF DIRECTORS OF

The first meeting of directors was held at

on the   day of   19   at   o'clock   M.

The following were present:

being a quorum and all the directors of the corporation.

One of the directors called the meeting to order. Upon motion duly made, seconded and carried,
was duly elected chairman of the meeting and
was duly elected secretary thereof. They accepted their respective offices and proceeded
with the discharge of their duties.

A written waiver of notice of this meeting signed by the directors was submitted,
read by the secretary and ordered appended to these minutes.

The chairman stated that the election of officers was then in order.

The following were duly nominated and, a vote having been taken, were unani-
mously elected officers of the corporation to serve for one year and until their successors
are elected and qualified:
President:
Vice-President:
Secretary:
Treasurer:

The president and secretary thereupon assumed their respective offices in place
and stead of the temporary chairman and the temporary secretary.

WAIVER OF NOTICE OF THE FIRST MEETING OF
THE BOARD OF DIRECTORS OF

_____

      We, the undersigned, being all the directors of the above corporation hereby agree and consent that the first meeting of the board be held on the date and at the time and place stated below for the purpose of electing officers and the transaction thereat of all such other business as may lawfully come before said meeting and hereby waive all notice of the meeting and of any adjournment thereof.

Place of meeting
Date of meeting
Time of meeting

_____
Director

_____
Director

_____
Director

Dated:

ORGANIZATION MINUTES OF THE SOLE DIRECTOR OF

_____

The undersigned, being the sole director of the corporation, organized under the General Corporation Law of Delaware, took the following action to organize the corporation and in furtherance of its business objectives on the date and at the place set forth below:

A certified copy of the Certificate of Incorporation filed in the office of the Secretary of State on   19   and recorded in the office of the Recorder of the County of   19 was appended to these minutes.

The office of the corporation was fixed at

in the City of   State of

By-Laws regulating the conduct of the business and affairs of the corporation were adopted and appended to these minutes.

It was decided to issue from time to time all of the authorized shares of the capital stock of the corporation, now or hereafter authorized, wholly or partly for cash, for labor done, or services performed, or for personal property, or real property or leases thereof, received for the use and lawful purposes of the corporation, or for any consideration, permitted by law, as in the discretion of the director may seem for the best interest of the corporation.

The following were appointed officers of the corporation to serve for one year and until their successors were appointed or elected and qualified:

President: Secretary:

Vice-President: Treasurer:

Each officer thereupon assumed the duties of his office.

A written proposal from addressed to the corporation and dated pertaining to the issuance of the shares of the corporation was appended to the minutes.

The following action was taken upon said proposal:

RESOLVED, that said proposal or offer be and the same hereby is approved and accepted and that in accordance with the terms thereof, the corporation issue to the offeror(s) or nominee(s)   fully paid and non-assessable shares of this corporation, and it is

RESOLVED, that upon the delivery to the corporation of said assets and the execution and delivery of such proper instruments as may be necessary to transfer and convey the same to the corporation, the officers of this corporation are authorized and directed to execute and deliver the certificate or certificates for such shares as are required to be issued and delivered on acceptance of said proposal in accordance with foregoing.

63

BY-LAWS
OF

ARTICLE I — OFFICES

SECTION 1. REGISTERED OFFICE. — The registered office shall be established and maintained at

in the County of   in the State of Delaware.

SECTION 2. OTHER OFFICES. — The corporation may have other offices, either within or without the State of Delaware, at such place or places as the Board of Directors may from time to time appoint or the business of the corporation may require.

ARTICLE II — MEETING OF STOCKHOLDERS

SECTION 1. ANNUAL MEETINGS. — Annual meetings of stockholders for the election of directors and for such other business as may be stated in the notice of the meeting, shall be held at such place, either within or without the State of Delaware, and at such time and date as the Board of Directors, by resolution, shall determine and as set forth in the notice of the meeting. In the event the Board of Directors fails to so determine the time, date and place of the meeting, the annual meeting of stockholders shall be held at the registered office of the corporation in Delaware on

If the date of the annual meeting shall fall upon a legal holiday, the meeting shall be held on the next succeeding business day. At each annual meeting, the stockholders entitled to vote shall elect a Board of Directors and may transact such other corporate business as shall be stated in the notice of the meeting.

SECTION 2. OTHER MEETINGS. — Meetings of stockholders for any purpose other than the election of directors may be held at such time and place, within or without the State of Delaware, as shall be stated in the notice of the meeting.

SECTION 3. VOTING. — Each stockholder entitled to vote in accordance with the terms and provisions of the Certificate of Incorporation and these By-Laws shall be entitled to one vote, in person or by proxy, for each share of stock entitled to vote held by such stockholder, but no proxy shall be voted after three years from its date unless such proxy provides for a longer period. Upon the demand of any stockholder, the vote for directors and upon any question before the meeting shall be by ballot. All elections for directors shall be decided by plurality vote; all other questions shall be decided by majority vote except as otherwise provided by the Certificate of Incorporation or the laws of the State of Delaware.

SECTION 4. STOCKHOLDER LIST. — The officer who has charge of the stock ledger of the corporation shall at least 10 days before each meeting of stockholders prepare a complete alphabetically addressed list of the stockholders entitled to vote at the ensuing election, with the number of shares held by each. Said list shall be open to the examination of any stockholder, for any purpose germane to the meeting, during ordinary business hours, for a period of at least ten days prior to the meeting, either at a place within the city where the meeting is to be held. Which place shall be specified in the notice of the meeting, or, if not so specified, at the place where the meeting is to be held. The list shall be available for inspection at the meeting.

SECTION 5. QUORUM. — Except as otherwise required by law, by the Certificate of Incorporation or by these By-Laws, the presence, in person or by proxy, of stockholders holding a majority of the stock of the corporation entitled to vote shall constitute a meeting, a majority in interest of the stockholders entitled to vote thereat, present in person or by proxy, shall have power to adjourn the meeting from time to time, without notice other than announcement at the meeting, until the requisite amount of stock entitled to vote shall be present. At any such adjourned meeting at which the requisite amount of stock entitled to vote shall be represented, any business may be transacted which might have been transacted at the meeting as originally noticed; but only those stockholders entitled to vote at the meeting as originally noticed shall be entitled to vote at any adjournment or adjournments thereof.

SECTION 6. SPECIAL MEETINGS. — Special meetings of the stockholders, for any purpose, unless otherwise prescribed by statute or by the Certificate of Incorporation, may be called by the president and shall be called by the president or secretary at the request in writing of a majority of the directors or stockholders entitled to vote. Such request shall state the purpose of the proposed meeting.

SECTION 7. NOTICE OF MEETINGS. — Written notice, stating the place, date and time of the meeting, and the general nature of the business to be considered, shall be given to each stockholder entitled to vote thereat at his address as it appears on the records of the corporation, not less than ten nor more than fifty days before the date of the meeting.

SECTION 8. BUSINESS TRANSACTED. — No business other than that stated in the notice shall be transacted at any meeting without the unanimous consent of all the stockholders entitled to vote thereat.

SECTION 9. ACTION WITHOUT MEETING. — Except as otherwise provided by the Certificate of Incorporation, whenever the vote of stockholders at a meeting thereof is required or permitted to be taken in connection with any corporate action by any provisions of the statutes or the Certificate of Incorporation or of these By-Laws, the meeting and vote of stockholders may be dispensed with, if all the stockholders who would have been entitled to vote upon the action if such meeting were held, shall consent in writing to such corporate action being taken.

ARTICLE III — DIRECTORS

SECTION 1. NUMBER AND TERM. — The number of directors shall be
The directors shall be elected at the annual meeting of stockholders and each director shall be elected to serve until his successor shall be elected and shall qualify. The number of directors may not be less than three except that where all the shares of the corporation are

owned beneficially and of record by either one or two stockholders, the number of directors may be less than three but not less than the number of stockholders.

SECTION 2. RESIGNATIONS. — Any director, member of a committee or other officer may resign at any time. Such resignation shall be made in writing, and shall take effect at the time specified therein, and if no time be specified, at the time of its receipt by the President or Secretary. The acceptance of a resignation shall not be necessary to make it effective.

SECTION 3. VACANCIES. — If the office of any director, member of a committee or other officer becomes vacant, the remaining directors in office, though less than a quorum by a majority vote, may appoint any qualified person to fill such vacancy, who shall hold office for the unexpired term and until his successor shall be duly chosen.

SECTION 4. REMOVAL. — Any director or directors may be removed either for or without cause at any time by the affirmative vote of the holders of a majority of all the shares of stock outstanding and entitled to vote, at a special meeting of the stockholders called for the purpose and the vacancies thus created may be filled, at the meeting held for the purpose of removal, by the affirmative vote of a majority in interest of the stockholders entitled to vote.

SECTION 5. INCREASE OF NUMBER. — The number of directors may be increased by amendment of these By-Laws by the affirmative vote of a majority of the directors, though less than a quorum, or, by the affirmative vote of a majority in interest of the stockholders, at the annual meeting or at a special meeting called for that purpose, and by like vote the additional directors may be chosen at such meeting to hold office until the next annual election and until their successors are elected and qualify.

SECTION 6. COMPENSATION. — Directors shall not receive any stated salary for their services as directors or as members of committees, but by resolution of the board a fixed fee and expenses of attendance may be allowed for attendance at each meeting. Nothing herein contained shall be construed to preclude any director from serving the corporation in any other capacity as an officer, agent or otherwise, and receiving compensation therefor.

SECTION 7. ACTION WITHOUT MEETING. — Any action required or permitted to be taken at any meeting of the Board of Directors, or of any committee thereof, may be taken without a meeting, if prior of such action a written consent thereto is signed by all members of the board, or of such committee as the case may be, and such written consent is filed with the minutes of proceedings of the board or committee.

ARTICLE IV — OFFICERS

SECTION 1. OFFICERS. — The officers of the corporation shall consist of a President, a Treasurer, and a Secretary, and shall be elected by the Board of Directors and shall hold office until their successors are elected and qualified. In addition, the Board of Directors may elect a Chairman, one or more Vice-Presidents and such Assistant Secretaries and Assistant Treasurers as it may deem proper. None of the officers of the corporation need be directors. The officers shall be elected at the first meeting of the Board of Directors after each annual meeting. More than two offices may be held by the same person.

SECTION 2. OTHER OFFICERS AND AGENTS. — The Board of Directors may appoint such officers and agents as it may deem advisable, who shall hold their offices for such terms and shall exercise such power and perform such duties as shall be determined from time to time by the Board of Directors.

SECTION 3. CHAIRMAN. — The Chairman of the Board of Directors if one be elected, shall preside at all meetings of the Board of Directors and he shall have and perform such other duties as from time to time may be assigned to him by the Board of Directors.

SECTION 4. PRESIDENT. — The President shall be the chief executive officer of the corporation and shall have the general powers and duties of supervision and management usually vested in the office of President of a corporation. He shall preside at all meetings of the stockholders if present thereat, and in the absence or non-election of the Chairman of the Board of Directors, at all meetings of the Board of Directors, and shall have general supervision, direction and control of the business of the corporation. Except as the Board of Directors shall authorize the execution thereof in some other manner, he shall execute bonds, mortgages, and other contracts in behalf of the corporation, and shall cause the seal to be affixed to any instrument requiring it and when so affixed the seal shall be attested by the signature of the Secretary or the Treasurer or an Assistant Secretary or an Assistant Treasurer.

SECTION 5. VICE-PRESIDENT. — Each Vice-President shall have such powers and shall perform such duties as shall be assigned to him by the directors.

SECTION 6. TREASURER. — The Treasurer shall have the custody of the corporate funds and securities and shall keep full and accurate account of receipts and disbursements in books belonging to the corporation. He shall deposit all moneys and other valuables in the name and to the credit of the corporation in such depositories as may be designated by the Board of Directors.

The Treasurer shall disburse the funds of the corporation as may be ordered by the Board of Directors, or the President, taking proper vouchers for such disbursements. He shall render to the President and Board of Directors at the regular meetings of the Board of Directors, or whenever they may request it, an account of all his transactions as Treasurer and of the financial condition of the corporation. If required by the Board of Directors, he shall give the corporation a bond for the faithful discharge of his duties in such amount and with such surety as the board shall prescribe.

SECTION 7. SECRETARY. — The Secretary shall give, or cause to be given, notice of all meetings of stockholders and directors, and all other notices required by law or by these By-Laws, and in case of his absence or refusal or neglect to do so, any such notice may be given by any person thereunto directed by the President, or by the directors, or stockholders, upon whose requisition the meeting is called as provided in these By-Laws. He shall record all the proceedings of the meetings of the corporation and of directors in a book to be kept for that purpose, and shall affix the seal to all instruments requiring it, when authorized by the directors or the President, and attest the same.

SECTION 8. ASSISTANT TREASURERS & ASSISTANT SECRETARIES. Assistant Treasurers and Assistant Secretaries, if any, shall be elected and shall have such powers and shall perform such duties as shall be assigned to them, respectively, by the directors.

ARTICLE V

SECTION 1. CERTIFICATES OF STOCK. — Every holder of stock in the corporation shall be entitled to have a certificate, signed by, or in the name of the corporation by, the chairman or vice-chairman of the board of directors, or the president or a vice-president and the treasurer or an assistant treasurer, or the secretary of the corporation, certifying the number of shares owned by him in the corporation. If the corporation shall be authorized to issue more than one class of stock or more than one series of any class, the designations, preferences and relative, participating, optional or other special rights of each class of stock or series thereof, and the qualifications, limitations, or restrictions of such preferences and/or rights shall be set forth in full or summarized on the face or back of the certificate which the corporation shall issue to represent such class or series of stock, provided that, except as otherwise provided in section 202 of the General Corporation Law of Delaware, in lieu of the foregoing requirements, there may be set forth on the face or back of the certificate which the corporation shall issue to represent such class or series of stock, a statement that the corporation will furnish without charge to each stockholder who so requests the powers, designations, preferences and relative, participating, optional or other special rights of each class of stock or series thereof and the qualifications, limitations or restrictions of such preferences and/or rights. Where a certificate is countersigned (1) by a transfer agent other than the corporation or its employee, or (2) by a registrar other than the corporation or its employee, the signatures of such officers may be facsimiles.

SECTION 2. LOST CERTIFICATES. — New certificates of stock may be issued in the place of any certificate therefore issued by the corporation, alleged to have been lost or destroyed, and the directors may, in their discretion, require the owner of the lost or destroyed certificate or his legal representatives, to give the corporation a bond, in such sum as they may direct, not exceeding double the value of the stock, to indemnify the corporation against it on account of the alleged loss of any such new certificate.

SECTION 3. TRANSFER OF SHARES. — The shares of stock of the corporation shall be transferable only upon its books by the holders thereof in person or by their duly authorized attorneys or legal representatives, and upon such transfer the old certificates shall be surrendered to the corporation by the delivery thereof to the person in charge of the stock and transfer books and ledgers, or to such other persons as the directors may designate, by who they shall be cancelled, and new certificates shall thereupon be issued. A record shall be made of each transfer and whenever a transfer shall be made for collateral security, and not absolutely, it shall be so expressed in the entry of the transfer.

SECTION 4. STOCKHOLDERS RECORD DATE. — In order that the corporation may determine the stockholders entitled to notice of or to vote at any meeting of stockholders or any adjournment thereof, or to express consent to corporate action in writing without a meeting, or entitled to receive payment of any dividend or other distribution or allotment of any rights, or entitled to exercise any rights in respect of any change, conversion or exchange of stock or for the purpose of any other lawful action, the Board of Directors may fix, in advance, a record date, which shall not be more than sixty nor less than ten days before the day of such meeting, nor more than sixty days prior to any other action. A determination of stockholders of record entitled to notice of or to vote a meeting of stockholders shall apply to any adjournment of the meeting; provided, however, that the Board of Directors may fix a new record date for the adjourned meeting.

SECTION 5. DIVIDENDS. — Subject to the provisions of the Certificate of Incorporation the Board of Directors may, out of funds legally available therefor at any regular or special meeting, declare dividends upon the capital stock of the corporation as and when they deem expedient. Before declaring any dividends there may be set apart out of any funds of the corporation available for dividends, such sum or sums as the directors from time to time in their discretion deem proper working capital or as a reserve fund to meet contingencies or for equalizing dividends or for such other purposes as the directors shall deem conducive to the interests of the corporation.

SECTION 6. SEAL. — The corporate seal shall be circular in form and shall contain the name of the corporation, the year of its creation and the words "CORPORATE SEAL DELAWARE." Said seal may be used by causing it or a facsimile thereof to be impressed or affixed or otherwise reproduced.

SECTION 7. FISCAL YEAR. — The fiscal year of the corporation shall be determined by resolution of the Board of Directors.

SECTION 8. CHECKS. — All checks, drafts, or other orders for the payment of money, notes or other evidences of indebtedness issued in the name of the corporation shall be signed by officer or officers, agent or agents of the corporation, and in such manner as shall be determined from time to time by resolution of the Board of Directors.

SECTION 9. NOTICE AND WAIVER OF NOTICE. — Whenever any notice is required by these By-Laws to be given, personal notice is not meant unless expressly stated, and any notice so required shall be deemed to be sufficient if given by depositing the same in the United States mail, postage prepaid, addressed to the person entitled thereto at his address as it appears on the records of the corporation, and such notice shall be deemed to have been given on the day of such mailing. Stockholders not entitled to vote shall not be entitled to receive notice of any meetings except as otherwise provided by statute.

Whenever any notice whatever is required to be given under the provisions of any law, or under the provisions of the Certificate of Incorporation of the corporation or these By-Laws, a waiver thereof in writing signed by the person or persons entitled to said notice, whether before or after the time stated therein, shall be deemed proper notice.

ARTICLE VI — AMENDMENTS

These By-Laws may be altered and repealed and By-Laws may be made at any annual meeting of the stockholders or at any special meeting thereof if notice thereof is contained in the notice of such special meeting by the affirmative vote of a majority of the stock issued and outstanding or entitled to vote thereat, or by the regular meeting of the Board of Directors, at any regular meeting of the Board of Directors, or at any special meeting of the Board of Directors, if notice thereof is contained in the notice of such special meeting.

WHAT TO DO WHEN AN EXISTING ESTABLISHED
BUSINESS INCORPORATES

SECTION XXII

There are some steps involved to transfer the financial records of a non-incorporated business to a corporation.

Below is a guideline to follow when a proprietorship or partnership becomes a corporation:

1. Arrange to form the corporation. If using a registered agent make this selection.

2. New books and records should be prepared to reflect the new corporate status and the corporation name.

   a. Decide whether to transfer accounts receivable* to the corporation and notify customers of the change. This is optional.

   b. Decide whether to transfer accounts payable* to the corporation and to notify creditors of the change.

   c. Decide whether to transfer capital assets* to the corporation.

   d. Decide whether to transfer inventory* to corporation records.

   e. Decide on the ending date of the corporate year to be used for income tax reporting purposes.

   f. Decide whether to notify all company associates and businesses dealt with as well as customers of the new corporate status. This can be done with sales producing advertising, and often, at no cost. Newspaper editors will usually run publicity of this new change on the financial page. An announcement by the owner(s) of the corporation should be typed and sent to the financial editor of the newspaper where the company's office is located.

3. Order new letterheads reflecting corporate name.

4. Open a bank account in the name of the corporation.

5. Transfer insurance policies to the corporation.

6. Arrange for any leases or other documents to be changed to reflect the corporation status.

7. Arrange to redo any employment contracts that exist with the old company, with the new corporation.

It would be helpful to counsel with an accountant and if there are complications with agreements, with a lawyer on handling the above details.

* If applicable.

SUGGESTED READINGS

SECTION XXIII

A list of the author's favorite readings is included. While having little or nothing to do with incorporating, they are recommended. Some are oriented toward business, others are philosophical or psychological in nature. All are possible aids in thinking, self-improvement, or formulating business ideas.

Branden, Nathaniel, THE DISOWNED SELF.
  Nash Publishing Co., Los Angeles, California

Caples, John, MAKING ADS PAY.
  Dover Press, New York, New York

Dible, Donald M., UP YOUR OWN ORGANIZATION.
  Entrepreneur Press, Santa Clara, California

Dible, Donald M., WINNING THE MONEY GAME.
  Entrepreneur Press, Santa Clara, California

Grant, Richard W., THE INCREDIBLE BREAD MACHINE.
  Academic Associates, Los Angeles, California

Greene, Gardiner, HOW TO START AND MANAGE YOUR OWN SMALL BUSINESS.
  McGraw-Hill Book Co., New York, New York

Hipple, G. Worthington, SELL YOURSELF RICH.
  Acropolis Books, Washington, D.C.

Hopkins, Claude, MY LIFE IN ADVERTISING.
  Crain Books, Chicago, Illinois

Joffe, Gerardo, HOW YOU TOO CAN MAKE AT LEAST $1 MILLION IN THE MAIL
  ORDER BUSINESS. Advance Books, San Francisco, California

Lane, Marc, LEGAL HANDBOOK FOR SMALL BUSINESS.
  American Management Association, New York, New York

Nicholas, Ted, HOW TO FORM YOUR OWN PROFESSIONAL CORPORATION.
  Enterprise Publishing Co., Wilmington, Delaware

Rand, Ayn, ATLAS SHRUGGED.
  Random House, New York, New York

Rand, Ayn, CAPITALISM: THE UNKNOWN IDEAL.
  Signal Books, The New American Library, New York, New York

Rosefsky, Robert, GETTING FREE: HOW TO PROFIT MOST OUT OF WORKING FOR
  YOURSELF. Quandrangle Books, New York, New York

Seltz, David, A TREASURY OF BUSINESS OPPORTUNITIES
  Farnsworth Publishing Co., Rockville Center, New York

Watkins, Julian L., 100 GREATEST ADVERTISEMENTS
  Dover Publications, New York, New York

White, Richard, THE ENTREPRENEUR'S MANUAL
  Chilton Book Co., Radnor, Pennsylvania

71

A few of the Companies that have already incorporated through this book —
From all 50 States and other countries throughout the world.

Name	Type of Business
AIDA Group Travel Coordinators & Travel Agents, Inc.	Group and individual travel to the general public
Airspeed Refinishing, Inc.	Custom painting of aircraft and other vehicles
Alaska Book Company	Book Sales
Allied Auto International, Ltd.	Services and delivery of foreign vehicles to U.S.A.
Amazing Diets, Inc.	Publishers
American Armed Forces Association	Fraternal servicemen's organization
The American Society of Child Advocates	Non-profit society to promote children's rights
Arundel Pool Management, Inc.	Management, opening, closing and maintenance of swimming pools
Balancing Act Corporation	Manufacture of weighing scales
The Balloon Company	Operate a balloon for hire
Better Builders & Remodelers, Inc.	Building and remodeling of residential and commercial buildings
Better Business Maintenance Co.	Janitorial and maintenance services
Bost Farms, Inc.	Farming
Calphil Corporation	Import-Export
Chronos, Incorporated	Financial planning
Cicero Cheese Manufacturing Corp.	Manufacture of cheese
Cindex Incorporated	Computer technical services
Covered Bridge Craft Barn and Garden Centre, Incorporated	Retail and wholesale sales of crafts, antiques, and plants through garden center
Creative Products, Inc.	Marketing organization
Criminal Justice Associates, Inc.	Consultations to Criminal Justice schools and agencies
The Cron Corporation	Printing, publishing and management services
Cultural Commercial Exchange, Inc.	Cultural/commercial centers and festival sponsorship
Dakota Nomad, Inc.	Bicycle and cross-country ski retail sales and manufacture of accessories
Denticare of Delaware, Inc.	Prepaid dental healthcare plan
Dexterity Unlimited, Inc.	Retail and wholesale sales and production of handcrafted items
Different Drummer, Inc.	Yacht charter
The Dinky Rink, Inc.	Roller skating
Doug's Aircraft Interiors, Inc.	Aircraft upholstery and accessories
Electron Optics Corporation	Manufacturing of surveillance equipment
Energy Independence Now, Inc.	Alternative energy sources
Eunitron, Inc.	Provide investment advisory service (publish a market letter)
European Overseas American, Inc.	Banking abroad, merchant banking
Excelsior International Corporation	Import and export
Fallbrook Ranchers, Inc.	Avocado and josoba nut ranching
Family Name Researchers, Inc.	Researching of surnames, family trees, genealogy, production of armorial bearings, etc.
Finance Corporation for Credit & Commerce	Financial and investment services
Flash Clinic Inc.	Service and repair of electronic flash equipment
Garon Enterprises, Inc.	Numismatics
Golconda Feed & Grain, Inc.	Agricultural products
Green Cargo, Inc.	Diversified sales of plants and accessories
Group Two, Inc.	Educational seminars
The Growing Concern, Inc.	Greenhouses, solar systems
Guardian Protective Coatings, Inc.	Applications and sales of protective coatings
Honey Creek Farm, Inc.	Livestock Farming
Hypertension Clinic, Inc.	Medical and health care, and teaching
Imperial Adhesives, Ltd.	Light manufacturing
Infinity's Child, Inc.	Decorating glass
Institute for Neuropsychopharmacologic Research, Inc.	Scientific research

Name	Type of Business
International Development Service Corp.	Export/import trade
International Geophysics, Inc.	Geophysical sales and services
Jetair, Inc.	Dealers in aircraft, flight instruction, and general aviation services
K & B Sink Tops, Inc.	Manufacturer of sink and counter tops
The Lighthouse Repertory Theatre, Inc.	Theatrical productions
Mafia, Inc.	Bumper stickers
Mountain Sales, Inc.	Redwood table sales (handmade)
Music Makers Unlimited, Inc.	Musical services, band and orchestra
Nova Hang Gliders, Inc.	Sales and service of hang gliders and accessories
OMV Corporation	Real estate
Old World Antiques Corporation	Wholesale and retail antiques
PeTaxi, Inc.	Rescue, receiving, air-shipping of pets, pet sitting, escort service for housepets
Pickwick Enterprises Corporation	Fish & Chips shop
Pineville Medical Clinic, Inc.	Health and medical service
Plane, Inc.	Transportation
Psychynotics Foundation	Research and teaching of hypnosis, mind control, metaphysics, psychic phenomena
R and B Logging Inc.	Timber logging
Rainsong Institute	Advocacy of efficient energy use
Red Dawn Productions, Inc.	Film Production
Reel Creations, Inc.	Music
Regina Careers, Ltd.	Self-training courses for home study
Scientific Resumes, Inc.	Polygraph testing
Seaboard Resources, Inc.	Management consulting and trading
Sign of the Times Corporation	Silk-screened garments
Simmons Industries, Inc.	Design, development, manufacture and sales of poultry processing and related equipment and supplies
Snowcrest Corp.	Horsebreeding and training
Sponsler-Nitrogen-Service, Inc.	Retail — fertilizer, chemicals and apply same
Stock Shot Corporation	Marketing curling and skiing equipment
Tectonics International, Inc.	Architecture, engineering, construction, development, and management services in U.S. and abroad
Texmark Corporation	Act as holding company for retail and wholesale operations of liquor and supermarkets, brewing industry
The Thomas Talin Company	Fragrance
Thor-Bred Health Food Corporation	Health food for thoroughbred horses and other animals
To Have and To Hold Shops, Inc.	Misses sportswear
Transcontinental International, Inc.	Coal and energy products, sales and production
Transprocess Manufacturing Marketing Support Corporation	Business, tax and economy advices
Undersea Life Sciences Corp.	Consulting services for diving/hyperbaric related industries
Union-Euro-Markt, Inc.	Investments
Virginia Pork Corporation	Commercial swine production
Whitehouse Foods, Inc.	Retail Grocery Store
Woodcat Investments, Inc.	Investments
World Amateur Backgammon Championships, Inc.	Promotion of backgammon and other tournaments
World Backgammon Federation, Inc.	Sanctioning body for backgammon tournaments and official players and promoters organization
World Business Investment, Inc.	Real estate investment, sales and business opportunities
World Cycle, Inc.	Motorcycle repair and sales
Xanthippe Corp.	Investments
Zoii, Inc.	Natural clothing, crafts, etc.

WHEN YOU DECIDE TO INCORPORATE
Receive the forms you need absolutely FREE!

A portfolio of current forms for your corporation including open, close, non-profit non-stock, confidential information form and detailed information for The Company Corporation services is available ABSOLUTELY FREE from The Company Corporation, Dept. Q-4, 725 Market Street, Wilmington, Delaware 19801. Please use the order form provided at the bottom of page.

Should you require any further information pertaining to your incorporating needs or the services provided by The Company Corporation, you may call direct and a customer service representative will be available to assist you.

Telephone (302) 575-0440

- -

Mail to: **The Company Corporation**
Corporation Center
Dept. Q-4
725 Market Street
Wilmington, Delaware 19801

Please send me, ABSOLUTELY FREE the "Forms and Information Package" described above.

Name _____

Company _____

Address _____

City _____

State _____ Zip _____

The Nicholas
President's Letter

Business and personal planning ideas exclusively for the corporation president

Ted Nicholas has helped many thousands form corporations easily and inexpensively. Now he has organized a brand new service.

THE NICHOLAS PRESIDENT'S LETTER is the only publication devoted to the business and personal needs of company Presidents and owners of businesses.

Will THE NICHOLAS PRESIDENT'S LETTER be useful to every company President? Probably it will. But less so for Presidents of giant corporations like General Motors and U.S. Steel who have large staffs to help them with every problem. This new publication is for Presidents of medium-sized and small companies. These, we believe, are the men and women who need guidance – especially if their company is growing, or just starting up.

This letter provided twice-monthly (24 issues yearly) business and personal guidance for the entrepreneur.

Subjects covered include:

- Investigating new businesses: Ten questions you must ask.
- New ways to raise money for risk capital . . . for expansion.
- Expanding your present business. When it's better **not** to grow.

- Does your business lend itself to mail order? How to find out—for very little money.
- Health care: You can make it **all** tax-deductible.
- Hiring the right people. How to fire the wrong ones. Ways a small business can attract better people—even against big-company competition.
- Taking full advantage of corporate tax benefits.
- Barter arrangements: They can save you big money. But watch out for two pitfalls.
- Launching your company while you still keep your present job.
- Tax loopholes: A continuing service prepared specifically for company Presidents and owners of small businesses.
- When your competitors are richer and bigger, you can **still** do nicely. How to make your competition work **for** you – no matter what they do!
- Guaranteed ways to pay less in Social Security taxes – and maybe pay nothing at all.

- Travel: how to go first class, and pay less. Spots still unspoiled. How to make sure that **every** trip for and your spouse is tax deductible.

- How to fight city hall – and win. Times when it's better not to fight.

- Ways to minimize customer resistance if you are forced to raise prices.

- The government regulations a President **must** observe – broken down according to the size of your business. Regulations you can probably ignore.

- Accounting for Presidents. What to ask your accountant. How to pick the right accountant for your business. Are your accounting fees too high? How to determine if your accountant is giving you the best tax advice.

Also included are:

In depth reports on broader subjects— For instance the energy crunch how does the alert President cope with and even profit from it.

Sometimes the in depth reports continue for several issues—as long as it takes to give all the needed information. If you commissioned such a report from a research organization, you would of course have to pay several thousand dollars for it minimum. (One such report will pay for The Nicholas Presidents Letter far into the next century!)

Questions and Answers – The editors and outside experts will answer your business and personal questions (without publishing your name, if you prefer privacy). Here again no need to pay an expensive consultant.

Presidents Profile – This will portray Presidents who a) are successfully coping with the same problems that are probably plaguing you, b) are willing to give their fellow Presidents the benefit of their ideas.

You risk nothing. You may cancel the Nicholas Presidents Letter any time during the life of your subscription. If you do you'll receive a prompt and courteous refund for the unused portion of your subscription.

You will receive an issue – twice a month, 24 issues a year. The purchase price is tax deductible.

To subscribe mail coupon below. Order today without obligation.

■■■■■■■■■■■■■■■■■■■■■■■■■■■■■■■■■■■■

To: The Nicholas Presidents Letter
c/o Enterprise Publishing Co.
Enterprise Plaza
Dept. QP - 94N
Two West Eighth Street
Wilmington, DE 19801

Enclosed is ☐ my check or money order
for $150.
Charge my ☐ Master Charge ☐ Visa
Card No. _____ Exp. Date_____
Signature _____

Name _____

Company_____

Address _____

City_____ State _____ Zip _____

The Most Astonishing Business Breakthrough of the Decade

Success in business — especially in your own business — is not easy. It takes hard work and it takes knowledge.

You can get help from books and cassettes. And many of them can be of assistance. Now you can have the help of a dynamic business course you can put to work for yourself without risk.

This unique course was developed through years of trial and effort. The author, Ted Nicholas, made . . . and lost . . . two fortunes before refining these techniques into the practical system that built his first million dollar company. The same system can build *your* fortune in less time than you ever thought possible.

You'll learn how to start a business without risking one cent of your money . . . How to turn a hobby into a business . . . Foolproof techniques for immediately sizing up the profit potential of a business for creating money making advertisements . . . for competing against larger companies . . . for choosing the best price for your product or service . . . choose a business that will prosper during periods of inflation and recession. Here is a partial list of what you will receive with this dynamic course.

The dynamic OPPORTUNITIES UNLIMITED course-between-covers features:

- 22 complete information-packed study-at-home sections . . .
- Self-testing workshop sessions after every section . . .
- Actual tear-out worksheets you can use in setting up your business . . .
- Clear, concise, to-the-point language . . .
- Easy-to-understand charts and diagrams . . .
- More than 500 large-format pages . . .
- Handsome, durable, hardcover bindings . . .

Here's an advance preview of OPPORTUNITIES UNLIMITED's contents:

- Section One: The Basic Principles. The primary secrets of success.
- Section Two: Starting Your Business Career. Includes the four myths you have to un-learn before you can begin a successful business.
- Section Three: 12 Gripes That Could Be Turned into Business Opportunities. You can put any one of these to use right now—or come up with your own!
- Section Four: Adding the Missing Ingredients. Shows you how to improve on any readily available product — and build a successful business around it.
- Section Five: Specialized Markets. How to make them work for you.
- Section Six: 10 Businesses Started by Solving Problems of Other Businesses. Reveals the secrets of some of America's most successful entrepreneurs.
- Section Seven: 10 Fortune-Making Opportunities in the Next 25 Years. Tells you how to spot tomorrow's million-dollar business today.

- **Section Eight: Essential Factors to be Considered in Selecting a Business.**
- **Section Nine: Planning Your Company's Goals and Image.** Shows you exactly how to plan the all-important Business Plan. (Complete worksheets included.)
- **Section Ten: Legal Considerations for Getting Started.** Save $1000s by following these simple guidelines on when you **don't** need a lawyer.
- **Section Eleven: Methods of Starting a Business — Including Part-Time, Franchising and Buying Out.** Find out which method is best for you.
- **Section Twelve: Financing Your Business.** Little-known sources revealed.
- **Section Thirteen: Sources of Business Information.** Many are actually free!
- **Section Fourteen: Bookkeeping and Accounting.** It's easier than you ever imagined — when we show you how. (Complete worksheets included.)
- **Section Fifteen: Control of Assets.** Techniques to make your company grow **fast.**
- **Section Sixteen: Profit Control.** How to predict profits in advance of sales.
- **Section Seventeen: Financial Leverage.** Demonstrates the powerful technique known as "Super Leverage" — and many more proven profit builders.
- **Section Eighteen: Personnel Leverage.** How to create your own organization from the ground up. (Complete worksheets included.)
- **Section Nineteen: Marketing Leverage.** How to advertise — **guaranteed** ideas.
- **Section Twenty: Tax Guidelines for Business.** Dynamic money-saving methods for minimizing the bracket at which income is taxes — and much, much more.

OPPORTUNITIES UNLIMITED: the only business course-between-covers that guides you step by step — from the drawing board stage to an established business. Now available for a thirty-day Trial Period.

There is nothing else like it available today. The Opportunities Unlimited course offers a uniquely dynamic approach to business based upon:

One-step-at-a-time guidance, clearly written and concisely presented. We'll take you from your present situation into a new business with specific start-to-finish instruction, and plain-spoken language that's free of jargon and "gobbledegook."

Easy-to-understand examples to illustrate each principle. We won't just tell you how to put your business on the road to success — we'll show you . . . . . . with examples drawn from real business situations.

Actual "workshop" sessions to measure your progress. Each section in your course-between-covers ends with an actual "work" session that will begin to create in you the skills, knowledge, and mind for business so necessary for success.

You CAN make a fortune by starting your own business — send for Opportunities Unlimited now and find out how!

Isn't it time you got started in your own business? Is there anything gained by waiting another minute?

I know from experience that you can do it. And I also know that if you don't take that first big step forward right now, you probably will never do it. Not tomorrow. And maybe not ever.

The decision is now yours to make. Our money-back guarantee is ironclad. There is absolutely no risk of any kind on your part.

You can order Opportunities Unlimited with the form provided from Enterprise Publishing Company on the following pages. The price for the comprehensive course is $85.00. Code 414 .

Books for Success

Choose from Our Library of "How To" Help for the Entrepreneur

How To Form Your Own
Professional Corporation
by Ted Nicholas

In-depth coverage of the subject of incorporation for the professional in any field. Reviews the specific advantages and possible disadvantages and explains the important elements to include for efficient planning. Authoritative but easily read, this book provides examples and models of the necessary documents and includes references and information for additional assistance.

Hardbound 8½ x 11   Code 407
Price $19.95

How To Get Out –
If You're In Over Your Head   *by Ted Nicholas*

An aid in developing financial knowledge for managing financial affairs, personal and business expenses, *and setbacks.* The information applies to all income levels. Bankruptcy is explained and discussed in full detail. This book also includes forms and instructions.

Hardbound 8½ x 11   Code 409
Price $12.95

How To Do Business Tax Free   *by Midas Malone*

A complete explanation of tax havens – Switzerland, Hong Kong, Liechtenstein, Cayman Islands, Panama, Bahamas, Bermuda, and many more. The facts are outlined in detail to work for any income level. Usable forms, names to contact and a complete cost breakdown of trusts and corporations are included.

Hardbound 8½ x 11   Code 406
Price $14.95

How To Self-Publish Your Own
Book & Make It A Best Seller
by Ted Nicholas

Contains all the author's secrets of taking writing to the next step – publishing, marketing and reaping all the rewards. Includes test marketing, determining selling price, reducing production costs, copyrighting, how to get free advertising and publicity, *and much more!*

Hardbound, 8½ x 11   Code 405
Price $14.95

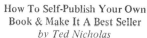

Where The Money Is
& How To Get It
by Ted Nicholas

How and where to raise money to finance a business, scholarship or research grant. Contains hundreds of sources of loans and capital. Complete with names, address and telephone numbers. Fully expanded listing includes venture capital firms, state sources, and selected banks. Techniques to save time and produce results. The most comprehensive book of its kind on the market today.

Hardbound 6 x 9   Code 402
ISBN 0913864 51 X   Price $12.50

Writing Part-time For
Fun And Money
by Jack Clinton McLarn

A valuable addition to the "How-to" field, a delightful, witty and charming book on and about writing, fun and money. This is a book that every person with an interest in writing needs at his fingertips. It will be a constant source of useful suggestions, moral support and inside information that no writer should be without.

Loaded with personal anecdotes from the author's own experience as a prolific freelance writer. A must for everyone who lifts pen to paper -- it covers:
- "Writing for Children and Kids" • Scripts • Reports
- Articles • Greeting Cards and other "Fringe Benefits"
- Confessions (or "Confessex")

And Much, Much More!

Hardbound 5½ x 8½   Code 412
ISBN 0913864 21 8   Price $9.95

How To Form Your Own Corporation
Without A Lawyer For Under $50
by Ted Nicholas

You can be the President of your own corporation quickly and easily, and at an amazingly low cost. This book is a "must" as a comprehensive reference guide for everyone's bookshelf. Thousands of people have incorporated using the system detailed in this book. Learn the many advantages of incorporating your business, hobby, or sideline. Large companies, small companies, and men and women who have part-time money making hobbies have done so. This exciting book shows you step-by-step how you can accomplish this for less than $50, and it contains all instructions, tear-out forms, and includes minutes, by-laws, and the actual certificate of incorporation.

Hardbound   Code 401   Price $14.95
Quality Paperback   Code 302   Price $5.95

How And Where To Raise Venture
Capital To Finance A Business   *by Ted Nicholas*
How to get the needed funds to start or expand a business. Unusual sources are revealed which are not commonly known, including 227 sources classified by individual to contact, address and telephone number. Information as to how to approach a capital source and various techniques of raising money. Tips to help prepare an effective financial proposal, and to determine start-up costs.

8½ x 11   Code 104
Price $9.95

Income Portfolio   *by Ted Nicholas*
Report describes a unique plan that shows how to convert most any job into a corporation. Includes forms and sample letter agreement. Enables user to increase take-home pay up to 25% without a change in job or salary. Employees and employers will find this report will be a useful guide in learning to operate a business with independent contractors. No payroll records or withholding taxes to maintain — all in compliance with IRS guidelines.

Over 100,000 copies in print
Quietly changing the face of American business

8½ x 11   Code 103
Price $9.95

How To Succeed In Your Own Business
by Ted Nicholas
Recorded live at the State University of New York at Albany, Ted Nicholas conducts a seminar on succeeding in one's own business. The tape is a full 78 minutes of useful, practical advice that listeners can put to immediate use. Contains step-by-step advice on getting a business started and raising capital; picking the right business and where the best opportunities are. An appropriate buy for people of all ages interested in succeeding in business.

Code 203   **Price $9.95**

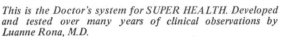

Enterprise Publishing Co., Inc.

Enterprise Plaza, Two West Eighth Street, Wilmington, Delaware 19801

Name _____

Address _____

City_____

State _____ Zip _____

☐ Check or Money Order Enclosed

Charge my account

    ☐ Visa   ☐ Master Charge

Card Number _____

Expiration Date _____

Signature _____

YES! Please send me the book(s) listed below. I understand that I may examine the book(s) for 14 days. If I am not fully satisfied for any reason, I may return them undamaged for a full refund of purchase price.

Quantity	Code	Title	Price	Total
	103	Income Portfolio	$ 9.95	
	104	How And Where To Raise Venture Capital To Finance A Business	9.95	
	105	How To Set Up Your Own Medical Reimbursement Plan	6.95	
	203	How To Succeed In Your Own Business (cassette tape)	9.95	
	302	How To Form Your Own Corporation Without A Lawyer For Under $50 (quality paperback)	5.95	
	401	How To Form Your Own Corporation Without A Lawyer For Under $50 (hardbound)	14.95	
	402	Where The Money Is And How To Get It	12.50	
	405	How To Self-Publish Your Own Book	14.95	
	406	How To Do Business Tax Free	14.95	
	408	Top Secret	2.95	
	409	How To Get Out—If You're In Over Your Head	12.95	
	412	Writing Part-time For Fun And Money	9.95	
	413	Total Glow	9.95	
	414	Opportunities Unlimited	85.00	
	497	How To Form Your Own Professional Corporation	19.95	

QP-01X

Grand Total _____

Cut along this line and mail